THINK IT CLEARLY,

MAKE IT TELL—

WITH INFORMATION IMPACT

THINK IT CLEARLY, MAKE IT TELL— WITH INFORMATION IMPACT

by

Frederick W. Harbaugh

THE CHRISTOPHER PUBLISHING HOUSE
NORTH QUINCY, MASSACHUSETTS

PRINTED IN

THE UNITED STATES OF AMERICA

To Gayla; she made this happen.

B.C. by permission of Johnny Hart and Field Enterprises.

Author's Preface

We English-speaking people have become so accustomed to inefficient verbal communication that most of us seem to expect it. Certainly most of us contribute to it, and we act as if we had no alternative. This phenomenon has troubled me since my childhood.

My previously passive concern about inefficient verbal communication became active when I read a magnificently simplistic observation by Rudolf Flesch in his book, *The Art of Clear Thinking* (Harper & Brothers, 1951). At the end of the chapter entitled "Robots, Apes, and You," Dr. Flesch says that thinking is simply "the manipulation of memories."

Suspecting a cause-effect relationship among memory manipulation, habit psychology, and communication efficiency, I began to inquire, experiment, and analyze: How do some people manage to communicate more efficiently than others? What do they do that makes their words meaningful and powerful? Do they do it consciously and, if so, what discipline do they follow? Could others be taught the same discipline? If so, how?

My interest in these questions was both intellectual and professional, and I have pursued my inquiry for more than twenty years. Finally I decided to write a guide to verbal communication efficiency based on my findings. This little book is the product of that decision and, I hope, a true reflection of its teaching. Confirming Solomon's venerable observation,[1] its substance is unoriginal; only its form is novel. And it is obviously unscholarly, since I am no scholar, but a practical, dogmatic industrial journalist. Accordingly, I offer here no recitation of my research, only a sweetened summary of my conclusions. It is, after all, more important to know how a tool is used than how it was made.

The book's title proclaims its theme, which centers around a body of seven principles that I promote professionally under the service mark Information Impact.[2] I think you will like the Information Impact system because:

1. It requires no specific education level or language aptitude, only functional literacy.
2. It asserts no rules or techniques, only principles.
3. It appeals to the mind; it solicits reason and habit.

In short, Information Impact is a simple, direct basis for clear thinking and vivid verbalizing. You can master it quickly and easily, as thousands of others are doing. When you do, it will incline you habitually to think, speak, and write more clearly, vigorously, and memorably, i.e., efficiently. It will do so by sharpening your awareness of the presence or absence of information.

The Information Impact principles are derived from established grammatical and rhetorical discipline, yet

---

1. " . . . there is nothing new under the sun" (Ecclesiastes 1:9).
2. Information Impact is a proprietary service mark of Frederick W. Harbaugh, letters patent applied for, U.S. Patent Office.

they carry no odor of the classroom. They are capsuled in crisp imperatives and set in a trim mnemonic pattern, so they are inviting to learn and easy to remember. They actually resist forgetting.

If your interest in clear thinking and verbal communication stops at the point of efficiency in the strict sense of that word (effectiveness without waste), you may wish to settle your advantage and press no further. And you will have a just reward. But people who learn to communicate efficiently often develop a strong secondary interest in correct pronunciation, spelling, and usage. For that reason I have complemented the Information Impact material with a chapter on popular errors, or solecisms.

Then, if your interest holds, you may wish to cultivate the niceties of idiom and style. Regarding that possibility I have included a chapter of counsel on those matters, following the chapter on solecisms.

Finally, if you have a vocational or serious amateur interest in verbal communication you will surely want to read further. Sensing that, I have added a chapter on books worth knowing, or at least knowing about. Here, as elsewhere, my views are not universally shared among literary people. But they are honest, traditional views, backed by classical authority and upheld by sound conservative practice.

Learning to use English efficiently and correctly requires effort, as it should. But the effort is easier than most people suppose, and the compensation is ample. Clear thinking and efficient communicating are acquired skills, not special gifts. They belong to those who earn them. May these pages help you do so.

I am grateful to Dr. Nelda R. Lawrence, Professor

Emerita of Business Technology, College of Technology, University of Houston, for reading this manuscript and suggesting numerous improvements, all of which have been incorporated. However, she is innocent of the judgments, inferences, and opinions expressed here: They are mine.

F. W. H.

Contents

11

THINK IT CLEARLY,

MAKE IT TELL—

WITH INFORMATION IMPACT

1

Tonguetied Thinking— English Broken Here

"O hateful error, melancholy's child!
Why dost thou show, to the apt thoughts
of men,
The things that are not?"
— *William Shakespeare (Julius Caesar)*

Probably no other literate people in the world communicate so badly as Americans.

We Americans blunt, blur, dissipate, distort, or dilute information almost every time we open our mouths or pick up a pencil. We do so habitually, unconsciously, even in our thinking. Most of us do so regardless of how well educated we are. Many of us do so who communicate professionally.

Much information conceived in English is inefficiently formed: its substance is cloudy, its point is dull, and its aim seems uncertain. Consequently, its impact is usually softened, and much of it misses its mark.

Why? The predominant cause is human habit—habitual negativism, indirectness, sterility, passiveness, pride, and porosity. I'll explain them further on. They, and not grammatical defect, cause most of our verbal communication inefficiency. They bear the blame for our words that say without telling.

Though functionally literate and often educated, many of us communicate inefficiently because we *think* inefficiently. And this is no mere reproach to our culture. It indicts our ideals, because—as information is the indispensable resource of enterprise—communication is the foundation of teamwork.

Unlike inefficient manufacturing, packaging, or distribution, communication inefficiency resists measurement. We know that it steals valuable time and invites tangible losses, and we see its shadow in depressed employee morale. But we have no means to measure it in dollars. We only know that it impairs operating efficiency, elevates operating costs, and erodes profits.

The cost to industry is surely substantial. Verbal communication inefficiency probably costs most American businesses as much as ten percent of their burden, taken as overhead plus general and administrative expense. It penalizes individuals heavily in their personal effectiveness, to the detriment of their career development and personal achievement. It costs everyone something.

I am convinced that much of this waste can be avoided by improving our interpersonal communication efficiency. To do so, however, we must find ways to make the information that we communicate more clear, vivid, unmistakable, and memorable, so that more of it will serve its purpose. But how may we do that: shall we practice candor and sincerity—say what we mean, and mean what we say? Shall we study literary style or formal rhetoric?

Certainly not. Candor is no match for ambiguity or equivocation, and sincerity makes a poor filter for unclear thinking. Our most candid and sincere comments are often misunderstood. As for literary style and rhetoric, some of our greatest literature communicates painfully, however entertaining or culturally valid it may be. Some of it is tedious to read.

Then possibly the answer lies in grammar? Again, no. Infinitive-splitting or ending a sentence with a preposition may offend English purists, but it seldom blunts the point of an otherwise sharp idea. And participle-dangling, though usually rustic, often brightens an otherwise dull one. Truly, grammatical purity offers no warranty of efficient communication.

No, information that is poorly conceived will be badly expressed. It will resist clarification by manners, morals, and mechanics. Do you wonder why? Easy: inefficient verbal expression reflects unclear thinking.

The Great Conspiracy

Our thinking, speaking, and writing habits are closely related; actually, they are interdependent. They are, in fact, psychologically inseparable and, as one psychologist puts it, "mutually reflective." They confirm and reinforce each other, fulfilling nature's design for consistency.

Consequently, if you form the habit of mumbling or slurring your speech, your carelessness will become evident in your thinking and writing. If you habitually favor negative expressions in your writing, your thinking and speech patterns will develop parallel negativisms. If you form the habit of reasoning circuitously, " 'round

Robin Hood's barn," your verbalizing will reflect it, independently of your knowledge or feelings about grammar, rhetoric, idiom, and style.

Habit is the most insistent phenomenon of nature. Your habits dominate your life; you deviate from them only by conscious effort or external persuasion. Therefore, realizing that communication is the key to successful interpersonal relationships, you probably would like to improve your communication habits—develop habits conducive to efficient communicating.

But powerful adversaries oppose you. Nature and circumstance have conspired against you. Nature inclines you to imitate others, and circumstance surrounds you with unworthy models. Influenced by nature and circumstance alone, you will almost certainly acquire habits that will predispose you to think, speak, and write inefficiently, regardless how earnestly and articulately.

Will It Hurt, Doctor?

How serious is this problem, really? Should the average citizen feel greatly concerned about it? If so, why? And is there an answer to it, a practical strategy against habits that are already deeply rooted in our psyches? The answers to those questions form both the cornerstone for my work as a public communication consultant, and my main thesis in this book. Those answers are, respectively, *very serious, yes, we'll go into that,* and *there is an answer* (you'll read it here).

The seriousness of verbal communication inefficiency is visible in its consequences, one of which, the penalizing of business operating efficiency and administrative economy, I mentioned earlier. But there are other, more personal consequences. When you instruct your spouse, child, garage mechanic, or attorney, you naturally intend your words to be persuasive and unmistakable. Failure to make yourself clear and cogent can spoil your afternoon, bring resentment or hostility, and invite embarrassment or expense.

As an employer, employee, neighbor, traveler, or telephone inquirer you will certainly wish to conserve your time, clarify your thoughts to others, and favor the probability that your thoughts, if not your exact words, are accurately remembered.

Thought-form Norms

The answer to inefficient verbal communication, the strategy for fighting it successfully, must address your habits in the deep recesses of your mind. That is, you must program your mind with norms conducive to efficient thinking—principles that promote the forming of sharply defined concepts. Implanted in your mind, and properly nurtured, such principles will displace unwholesome habits and bless your mind with intuitive clarity and vigor. Thus programed, your mind will subconsciously seek ways to shape and express your thoughts efficiently.

Of course, normative principles are merely guides, not rigid rules. Like your other habits, they will predispose you without denying your freedom of choice; and you should follow them confidently when you have no special reason to deviate. Principles in that sense, norms that suggest right action, are essential to efficient communicating.

Such are the principles of Information Impact, and there are only seven.

Taming the Game

The chapter that follows discusses these principles individually and in summary. It is, in fact, a kind of minibook with all nonessentials omitted.

Before you read it, let me suggest a proven, profitable way to exploit Information Impact. Determine to make all seven principles your personal norms for thinking and verbalizing; but make no attempt to swallow them whole at one sitting. If you try to assimilate them all at once you will get little benefit from them. Instead, adopt them one by one. Concentrate on a single principle each week for seven weeks, focusing your attention on each principle in turn.

Do this and you will grow sharper in information-awareness as you develop a habitual concern for efficient communication.

Resolve to make the Information Impact principles your permanent norms for thinking and verbalizing, and you will crystallize a lifelong business and social advantage. If you care to pursue your communication advantage into the realms of correctness and style, you can have no firmer foundation than the Information Impact principles.

2

Information Impact—
Freedom in A Framework

"There can be no economy where there is
no efficiency."

—Benjamin Disraeli (Letters, to
Constituents, 3 October 1868)

To communicate efficiently it is needless to master
English grammar, forfeit your sense of humor, or conquer your regional or ethnic accent (if you have one).

To communicate efficiently it is, however, necessary
to express ideas effectively without waste; and doing so
requires a certain discipline. Naturally, if the discipline
is to serve a large number of people it must be simple,
practical, and appealing. And it must transcend the
habits that incline us to communicate inefficiently.

I saw the need for such a discipline most poignantly
one day in 1955 when one of my associates chided me for
a remark that I suppose most Americans utter several

times daily. I know he was only half serious, but he jolted me into studying the nature of efficient verbal communication. He had asked me, "Do you think it's going to rain this afternoon?" And I had replied, "I don't think so." Scowling, he rebuked me, "Fred, I want to know what you *do* think." Well, as Solomon or someone aptly wrote, "Faithful are the wounds of a friend . . . " (Proverbs 27: 6). But I probably neglected to thank C. Joseph Zohn at the time, so I thank him now. His comment motivated me to develop and systematize the seven principles that I now promote under the service mark Information Impact.

These are the seven principles that in my opinion govern verbal communication efficiency. See them for what they are: merely principles. Make a place for them in your thinking, speaking, and writing. Encourage them to take root in your mind, and they will do so, to your everlasting advantage.

Practicing these principles will help you tremendously to think clearly, speak plainly, and write so that people understand and remember what you said. That's communication efficiency.

Principle One: *Posit*

Pronounce it *PAHZ-it*, like the first two syllables of *positive*; and that's a clue to the idea. It's an imperative, a command to express your ideas in positive form. That is, say what is, not what's not. Say what was, not what wasn't. Say what will be, not what won't be. And so on.

Here is an excerpt from an audit report, one of industry's drearier necessities:

" . . . We are not able to determine from these data

whether the pressure tests were valid . . . we do not
believe that the results are conclusive . . . we do not
believe the test data are fully set forth. . . . "

Industrial and government employees often talk and
write like that, and you can bet that they also think like
that. See what the little excerpt says. First it tells something that the writer and his associates cannot do; next it
tells some of the things they do not believe. We can see
how the writer feels about the test data, but his words—
the images of his thoughts—lack definite shape and sharp
focus. The more closely you look at them, the less they
seem to say.

They reflect the empty shell of an idea turned inside
out. They raise an absurd question: might it help to
know more of the things the writer cannot do, or more
of the things he does not believe?

Consciously or not, readers and listeners want to know
what writers and speakers *are* able to do—what they *do*
believe. If the writer of the audit report had known and
followed the *posit* principle he might have written, with
much greater impact and relevance:

" . . . We are unable to determine from these data
whether the pressure tests were valid . . . we believe
that the results are inconclusive . . . we suspect that
the test data are incompletely stated. . . . "

Positive expression sounds vigorous and confident.
Negative expression sounds almost wishy-washy in com-
parison. You can think of situations that practically
demand negative expression, of course; so can I. Many
of them occur in poetry. Some arise in political diplo-
macy. Others occur where you want to show both sides

of an idea for contrast or emphasis. But those are all special cases. Most ideas are sharper in positive form, including ideas that are essentially negative.

Maybe you're wondering why positive form is usually better than negative form. It's a fair question.

Positive information strikes the mind with greater force than negative information because it's affirmative. That makes it more definitive, more meaningful, and more memorable than negative information. The human mind instinctively seeks affirmative information and prefers it to negative information.

The product of negative expression, which might properly be called noninformation, is self-discounting. How helpful is it, generally, to learn what is not, was not, or will not be? Or what someone does not, did not, or will not do? The mind prefers better information: what is, was, or will be—what people do, did, or will do. And English idiom stands ready to satisfy that demand.

But what about our popular expressions like *not bad*, *not good*, *not happy*, *not well*, and *not at home*? Negative expression has a kind of recreational value in our casual conversation, especially where it serves the purpose of wit, humor, irony, sarcasm, emphatic understatement, or diplomatic evasiveness. However, the principle stands firm. In using negative form we should compromise a norm, not exercise one.

It's a perverse inconsistency that while our minds instinctively seek affirmative information, our speech—reflecting our thinking—seems often disposed to utter negative information. There is no logical reason, I believe, why most of us are more likely to say "I don't feel well" than "I feel ill"; no logical reason why we'll more probably say "not now" than "later." And surely no logical reason why so many of us will say "I don't think so" rather than "I think not" or "I doubt it."

But we are so inclined, to the detriment of efficient verbal communication; and our best hope seems to be to cultivate a positive norm.

For yourself, resolve now to cultivate the habit of positive expression. Sensitize yourself to positive-negative polarity in your reading and listening, and of course in your thinking, speaking, and writing. Make yourself *not*-sensitive.

Almost invariably you can find, if you look, a fitting positive way to express negative ideas. Instead of saying that something is "not acceptable," you can say that it is "unacceptable." Instead of saying "not very often," you can say "seldom." Instead of saying "I'm not going," you can say "I'm staying home."

But where you truly prefer it, for whatever reason, you can use negative form knowingly, fearlessly, and unapologetically. Just use it selectively, not habitually.

If you want to communicate more tellingly and efficiently, accentuate the positive. *Posit.*

Principle Two: *Assert*

Here is a standard English verb to which I have given a new arbitrary meaning: to state boldly and forthrightly.

Assert an idea and you show confidence and perspective. Lead up to it circuitously, beat around the bush, hesitate in any way, and you discount your idea. Read the following memorandum to the office staff of a Texas corporation:

Subject: Growth of Our Houston Office

From: Branch Manager

As you know, our staff has nearly doubled in recent years, and our growth has brought both prosperity and problems. The number of accounts that we serve has more than doubled, and our volume has tripled. Consequently, our future looks brighter than ever. However, we have added three new services, two of which bring customers to our office in the early and late hours of the day; and our customers' vehicles often overflow their allotted spaces in our parking lot.

I know that you share my desire to give our customers the best possible service. It benefits all of us to keep our customers happy. For another two years, at least, I expect our prosperity and our problems to increase. After that, when we occupy the new quarters that are being designed for us, we can expect some relief from the problems.

Meanwhile, we must make the best of our circumstances, and I will appreciate your cooperation with the following facts. This weekend we're going to enlarge our customer parking area, and this will reduce the space available for employee parking. This means that hereafter you will have added incentive to get to work on time. Actually, we're going to have to be more punctual anyway, because of our early and late customer activity. So we're going to have to expect all employees to be at their desks and ready to start work no later than 8:30 a.m., and to leave the work area no later than 5:30 p.m., except with my special approval.

Also, we're going to have to stagger lunch hours so

that our customers can be served promptly throughout the workday. And we're going to have to respect the lunch hours the same as the shift hours. Details about the lunch hours will be given to you through your supervisors. I know that you will cooperate with these requirements for the advantage of our company and the security of your employment.

(Signature, branch manager)

By the time you reached the heart of that memorandum you had read nearly two hundred words of preamble, and you may have wondered whether the writer spoke from conviction or mere duty. Try to remember the points of the message, and you are unlikely to recall them clearly in context or in sequence. As an employee you would be unlikely to take the new rules as seriously as the manager should have intended.

Had the manager been more *assert*ive he might have composed a much clearer and more compelling instruction, perhaps like this:

Subject: Punctuality, Lunch Hours, and Parking

From: Branch Manager

Starting Monday, 18 June, three new rules will be enforced uniformly at our Houston office:

1. *Shift punctuality.* Everyone must be at this desk and ready for work by 8:30 a.m., and no one may leave the work area before 5:30 p.m. without my approval.
2. *Lunch hour.* Everyone must follow the new lunch schedule, which is posted on the bulletin board. Exceptions will require my approval.
3. *Parking.* Additional spaces are being designated

for customer parking, and employees are forbidden
to use them during office hours.

These rules reflect our prosperity, and we should be
glad that we need them. We must maintain high
standards of customer service, and a disciplined company image, as we grow. I know you will agree that
this is a fair price to pay for secure employment.

(Signature, branch manager)

It is seldom if ever advantageous to pussyfoot. It is
almost always better to get straight to the point. Then,
if explanation or elaboration is needed, supply the details.
This is neither rude nor undiplomatic; it is courteous and
considerate. It spares the reader or listener the labor
of digging and sifting to find the core of your message,
and it favors the prospect of his understanding it clearly.

Here is a flagrantly pussyfooting letter from a timid
industrial buyer to a delinquent supplier:

Gentlemen:

As you know, we have bought most of our bronze
sheet from your mill since 1948. Your sheet has been
generally satisfactory, and we have had equitable ad-
justment of the few problems we have had with it.
However, we observe that your recent shipments have
grown increasingly late, and our production schedules
cannot tolerate the continuance of this pattern. . .

Obviously the buyer would have better served both his
employer and the vendor by writing bluntly:

Gentlemen:

We can accept no further late shipments of bronze
sheet under our Purchase Order No. 85361 and must

proceed to qualify alternate sources. Please contact us immediately if you can assure us of prompt future deliveries . . .

To communicate efficiently you must learn to *assert*. A point worth making is worth making bluntly. So, when you have something to say, say it straight out. Get right to the point; then explain if you must. Usually it's easier to explain a hard assertion clearly stated, than to clarify a muddy idea.

When you want to say something, step right up to it. Speak up. Get to the point. *Assert*.

Principle Three: *Personalize*

Learn to people your ideas. Give them life; inject personality. When you give information the appearance of personal presence you give it vitality. This is my own favorite principle: *Personalize*.

Everyone knows that oral speech communicates more clearly than written speech. Facial expressions, body gestures, voice intonations, and immediate feedback magnify the clarity and impact of oral speech. Even where the speaker and hearer are visually isolated from each other, so that instantaneous feedback is impossible (as in radio broadcasting), oral speech communicates more vividly than written speech.

Usually it is impossible to communicate as efficiently in writing as in oral speech because the speaker's personal absence attentuates his information. How this happens we can leave to psychologists. We know that it has something to do with personal presence, or visible personality, as a catalyst for the communication process.

There is a powerful reason why you should try always to *personalize* your messages, particularly your written ones. Remember that words have no intrinsic meanings. Meanings are simply the images that words call to mind. Thus, meanings are in people, not words. To summon vivid, memorable images to your reader's mind you must recognize and address your reader's personality, exhibit your own personality, and establish a human link for your reader's response.

Have you ever read this kind of letter:

Gentlemen:

Enclosed are corrected invoices for shipments forwarded under [company name] Purchase Order No. 36452. It is regretted that cost escalation has necessitated these price adjustments. Prompt acknowledgment is requested.

The message is clear enough, of course; but it sounds brutally cold, sterile, and impersonal. It mocks the signature beneath it. Compare it with this one:

Gentlemen:

Here are corrected invoices for recent shipments under your Purchase Order No. 36452. We hate to raise our prices, but our increased costs make it necessary. Please acknowledge these invoices right away, so we'll know that this is agreeable with you.

Injecting personality into messages is very simple. You just insert personal references—nouns, pronouns, and organic adjectives that reflect the you-and-me situation. They are, of course, less poignant than visible grimaces and audible voice intonations, but they help a lot.

Surprisingly few people know this, but the United States Army, Air Force, Bureau of Land Management, and other Federal and state government agencies officially advocate the *personalize* principle in explicit instructions to their employees. But tradition yields slowly and, as François de la Rochefoucauld observed a hundred years ago, hypocrisy is the fitting homage from vice to virtue. Accordingly, in practice you will find little personality in government prose.

Does that imply that third-person language is wrong? Certainly not. It has its place in legal writings, diplomatic correspondence, scientific reports, and other purposely contrived works. But third-person language makes a bad norm. It makes a more fitting exception. It's no harder to say "Will you please . . . " than "It is requested . . . ," and it communicates far more vividly.

What if you're a victim of institutional style or a superior's personal bias against personal language? Make the best of it and keep testing the boundaries. Some walls have cracks, and others will crumble under assault. If you are strictly forbidden to communicate humanly, try to be patient and watch your options.

We are by nature *persons*: we like to be recognized as such, addressed by our names, designated by personal pronouns, and talked *with* rather than *at*. Therefore, try always to address your ideas to people, not merely to other ideas. Strive toward a comfortable, dignified you-and-me attitude. You can be both personal and correct. Use plenty of I's, we's, you's, me's, etc. Doing so will make your ideas seem to live and breathe, and will make your communication more efficient.

Make it your norm to address people in writing as you do in speech—personally. *Personalize.*

Principle Four: *Activate*

This one has a slight tinge of grammar about it, but I promise you'll find it simple and painless. It commands you to make your ideas as forceful and direct as you can. That is, avoid the passive voice. Favor the active voice. In a word, *activate*.

Don't feel embarrassed if you've forgotten the meaning of active voice and passive voice. Some journalists seem to have forgotten. However, the distinction is clear and logical.

The two voices are aptly named. The active voice tells who does what to whom. It expresses direct action in the pattern of subject-verb-object, as in "The President vetoed the bill." The passive voice inverts the idea and tells what is done to whom *by* whom (and sometimes even omits the by whom). It expresses indirect action in the pattern of object-verb-subject, as in "The bill was vetoed by the President."

The passive voice is not necessarily bad, of course. It's needed where you want to give prominence to an object in preference to its subject, as in the headline, GOLD DISCOVERED BY HIKERS. And it's appropriate where you wish to subordinate (or even conceal) the doer of the action. But the passive voice tends to become habit-forming, and it makes an undesirable norm. Newspaper people are especially prone to passive-voice addiction, which sometimes injects unintended humor into otherwise drab reporting.

Early in 1971 a large daily newspaper printed a story under the headline, BOYCOTT IS REQUESTED OF QUAKER OATS BY SPORTSMEN'S CLUB. The writer may have believed that the concept of boycott has more luster than the concept of sportsmen or Quaker Oats; but more likely the writer was merely addicted to the passive voice. I believe the headline would have communicated more efficiently had it said SPORTSMEN THREATEN OATS BOYCOTT, using the active voice. However, the passive voice would have seemed entirely fitting if the story were suited to a headline like SEX ORGY DENIED BY SPORTSMEN.

The passive voice has its ugliest and least defensible abuses in business and industrial correspondence, including instructions to employees, where clear thinking and cogent communication are most urgently needed. Here are several for-instances from contemporary organizations:

"Defective paint coatings were found on nearly half of the flanges by the line inspectors."

"Increased profits are expected to be produced by the new cost reduction program."

"Expense vouchers must be submitted within thirty days by all route salesmen."

Now turn them around and see for yourself: The active voice communicates more tellingly—more efficiently.

In much the same way as the mind prefers affirmative to negative information, it prefers its information in the order of subject-verb-object, who does what to whom. People hear most attentively and read most interestedly what their minds prefer to receive, and that is direct action.

I have been trying to sell you the idea that the active voice is usually preferable to the passive voice, as I know it is. Not invariably, of course; just usually. Let me suggest that you become *by*-sensitive in the same way as I suggested that you become *not*-sensitive. Except where it is used to mean adjacence, the word *by* is most often found in passive sentence construction. Avoid it. Learn to think in the active voice, and make it your norm.

My favorite illustration to show how the passive voice saps ideas of their vogor and impact is a switch on an old adage of show business, thus: Don't let us be called by you; you'll be called by us.

The point is clear. *Activate.*

Principle Five: *Familiarize*

To be clearly and efficiently communicated, information must be imparted in terms familiar to the reader or listener. Therefore, you should make it your norm to *familiarize.*

Someone has suggested that educated men ought to "read up," "talk across," and "write down." That is, read "up" to broaden your knowledge and expand your vocabulary, talk "across" on the ground of known mutual understanding, and write "down" to the probable comprehension level of readers whom you may never meet. Done properly, writing down is never patronizing or condescending; it is courteous and considerate.

Most of us have four distinct vocabularies. First and smallest is our *speaking* vocabulary. It includes only the words we feel most comfortable with, and whose correct pronunciation we feel sure of. Second, and considerably larger, is our *writing* vocabulary. It includes many words whose correct pronunciation we feel unsure of, or which seem too formal for conversation, but whose meanings we understand. Third, and still larger, is our *listening* vocabulary. It includes many words whose generic meanings we know or can sense fairly well, but which we hesitate to repeat. Fourth, and largest of all, is our *reading* vocabulary. It includes words that we have no idea how to pronounce correctly, but whose generic or probable meanings we can sense from their spelling and context.

Unfortunately, your speaking and writing vocabularies may include words or phrases beyond the listening and reading vocabularies of others. If you're trying to make an idea clear to someone else, you're the one who takes the risk. The safe practice is to address others on the levels of *their* vocabularies; and the less you assume, the better for efficient communication.

Suppose you're an advertising distributor and you're drafting instructions to your handbill crew, most of whom are grade school students or transient adults. If you have a B.A. in sociology and are unaccustomed to considering others' communication problems you may begin something like this:

> Upon receipt of your distribution materials, boundary description, and street map, immediately verify that the supplied handbill count corresponds approximately to the logistics notation on your contract voucher. Report significant anomalies to the undersigned.
>
> Make unit delivery to the principal streetward entry point at each domicile within your boundary description. Be aware that multiple delivery to any entry point is forbidden, as is the willful discarding of handbills.
>
> Regard the indicated completion hour for your deliveries, and present your signed and dated contract voucher to the undersigned . . .

Now suppose your instructions are printed just as you drafted them. When you give a copy to a new crew member who just came to town from the hill country, and whose language is better suited to beekeeping than advertising, he will deserve great sympathy. And you will deserve twenty lashes with a significant anomaly.

The illustration may be a bit overdrawn, but instructions of that kind are fairly common at every level of our society. Rewriting them in familiar terms is good exercise; it's helpful to visualize and describe photographs or drawings that would illustrate your words, emphasizing small details.

The *familiarize* principle is probably the easiest to understand and the most difficult to apply of the Information Impact series. Perhaps you can see that it's difficult for *me*. If we're interested in communicating it's our nature to expand our vocabularies and exhibit their contents. But we need to remember that our communication grows less efficient with every foreign, exotic, pedantic, technical, or otherwise uncommon word that we utter.

Therefore, it's a wise resolve to avoid the needless use of such words and, where they're truly appropriate, make certain to clarify their meanings by defining them, picturing them, or revealing them in unmistakable context. In general it's best to favor the simplest, shortest, most familiar words that are both correct and adequate for your purpose.

Make a game of it until you form the habit. You're sure to win. *Familiarize.*

Principle Six: *Quantify*

Here is a possibly unfamiliar word. Pronounce it *QUANT-if-eye*. It simply means to express measurable ideas in measured words, that is, say *how much*.

If you studied engineering or science you learned to

quantify when you were in school, which makes you a member of a privileged minority group. Even so, outside your professional field you're probably a habitual nonquantifier like most of us. You're probably a habitual user of vague adjectives like hot, cold, long, short, high, low, expensive, cheap, etc.

The needless or inappropriate use of such words is like taking the elevator without indicating your floor, or flying north without a destination. The *too little/all right/too much* scale of values is useful for quick decision-making, but it leads to inefficient communication.

When we speak of a hot afternoon, a long journey, or a small farm, we could almost as easily—and with greater information impact—say that the temperature was 95° F, it was a 600-mile drive, and the farm was about eight acres.

But is it always desirable to *quantify*? Certainly not. Some qualities defy quantification in laymen's language, and others (for example, lovely, fragrant, and appealing) are unquantifiable. And there will be situations where, for one reason or another, you prefer to give only relative information.

Usually, however, failure to quantify defeats communication efficiency. Cultivate the habit of *quantify*ing wherever you can. Instead of saying "overstocked," say "320 in stock, 200 required." Instead of saying "capital squeeze," say "capital shortage of $125,000." Instead of saying "high-salaried employees," say "employees earning more than $20,000."

Where you can't *quantify*, try to limit. In the examples given immediately above you could say, respectively, "overstocked more than 50%," "capital shortage exceeding $100,000," and "employees at staff level and above."

You can see how simple and sensible it is to *quantify*. It favors the clear communication of useful information.

Tell a traveler, "Dallas is north of Houston," and you orient him. Tell him "Dallas is 260 miles north of Houston on U.S. Highway 75," and you give him what he needs.

Try to remember to say how much. *Quantify.*

Principle Seven: *Condense*

This is the common verb meaning to make denser or more compact. The more you *condense* an idea, the more succinctly you express it, the greater its impact.

Uncondensed information communicates less efficiently than condensed information because it offers the reader or listener an unwelcome choice: He can accept the burden of sifting or distilling to get the essential information, or he can disregard the message. Either way, the writer or speaker pays for his neglect. If the message is communicated at all, it is likely to lose something in the process and perhaps be remembered unclearly. And, of course, the writer or speaker may be remembered unfavorably.

Information can be condensed in two ways. But before we discuss them let's distinguish clearly between the words *condense* and *abbreviate.* You condense information by boiling it down. You abbreviate information by cutting it short. Condensed information takes less space than uncondensed information because it has been distilled, not amputated.

The two ways to condense information are:

1. Weed out the irrelevant.
2. Eliminate the needless.

Sounds simple, doesn't it? It is simple. The hard part is recognizing the need to do it. Usually the greatest obstacle is pride; we hate to admit that our habits need improving, so we resist making the effort. However, very few writers or speakers, if any, are disciplined enough to express any idea spontaneously without some irrelevant or needless information.

I am not suggesting that all needless information should be ruthlessly deleted from every message. Sometimes you can improve clarity and retention by deliberately inserting words that comfort the mind as it labors to comprehend an idea. Such words and phrases—like *however, in fact, of course*, and *nevertheless*—bridge gaps where our minds need verbal steppingstones. And sometimes repetition or paraphrasing is desirable to clarify or emphasize complex instructions.

But the irrelevant has no excuse other than, perhaps, occasional deliberate insertion to divert attention or becloud information. Unethical businessmen sometimes insert irrelevant information in reports or contracts for that purpose.

A friend of mine drafted the following letter to a Texas retailer whose computer had sent him several erroneous billing statements:

Gentlemen:

I have written to you about this problem twice before, and you have not yet answered my letters. I have been a regular customer of your stores for nearly twenty years, and I have always paid my bills promptly. I have never had an overdue account and never been accused of it until this problem came up.

As I have already told you, I have paid you everything I owe you, and I have the canceled checks to prove it. What I need now is your acknowledgment that your records are in error, and your assurance that

you will correct them without delay and without ad-
verse effect on my credit. If you fail to give me this
satisfaction, which is entirely reasonable to ask, I want
you to close my account, and we will just have to let
our attorneys decide what to do next.

                                                    (Signed)

My friend showed me his draft, and after discussing it
we rewrote it, deleting the irrelevant and needless, and
shaping it up a bit. Here is the revised letter:

Gentlemen:
   Please close my account, acknowledge its closure,
and send me your closing statement.
   You may reopen my account as soon as you correct
your records and rescind your libels against my credit.
My attorney has asked me to give you till 27 March.

                                                    (Signed)

My friend got action by return mail. Businessmen like
their information 100 proof, undiluted, and it pays to
serve it that way.

Beyond facts and ideas you can condense information at
the level of words and phrases. For example, many adjectives and adverbs are excess baggage; often you can
sharpen a message by withholding them. In case you've
forgotten, adjectives, such as sweet or sour, modify nouns,
such as orange or lemon. Adverbs, such as sweetly or
sourly, modify verbs, adjectives, or other adverbs, and
commonly (but not always) end in *ly*. Use adjectives and
adverbs selectively and sparingly, and you'll communicate more efficiently.

Most of us habitually pepper our speech with puffed-up
phrases that say no more than equivalent single words.

To fight the habit, here is a doctrine that anyone can learn: Never send a phrase to do a word's job. Here are several puffed-up phrases you should avoid—just samples of their kind:

Phrase	Equivalent word
On a weekly basis	Weekly
In a proper manner	Properly
With regard to	About
In the event that	If
In order to	To
At this point in time	Now (or currently)
Period of time	Time (or period)
. . . is a reflection of	Reflects
. . . has a tendency	Tends

Don't try to compile a list of such phrases; you'd never finish. But see the principle involved, and make it your habit.

And don't worry about sounding abrupt. The risk is greater that you'll fail to wring the water out of your ideas. Just remember the goal, which is to favor the relevant and necessary, and suppress the irrelevant and needless. Where surgery is indicated, use the knife.

In short, try to make every word tell. *Condense.*

Freedom For-ward

You now possess seven priceless principles of efficient communication. They can emancipate you as they have emancipated others. But the freedom they offer is *for* something, not *from* something. It is freedom to think more clearly and verbalize more efficiently.

These principles are vital to vivid, cogent expression.

All are good, yet none should be followed blindly. Exercise judgment when you use them. But whatever you do, make these principles your norms—your guides to right action.

Here they are in capsule form:

> *Posit*—Say what is, not what's not
> *Assert*—Get to the point, don't lead up to it
> *Personalize*—Address people, not ideas
> *Activate*—Favor the active voice: subject-verb-object
> *Familiarize*—Favor familiar words and phrases
> *Quantify*—Say how much
> *Condense*—Make every word tell

Chapter 1 closed with suggestions how to commit these principles to your personal habits. It suggested that you concentrate on one principle each week for seven successive weeks, drilling them into your mind with visual reminders and constant practice. It might help you to reread chapter 1 at this point.

One thing I know: when those principles settle into your habitual way of thinking, you'll find that you have a heightened sense of information awareness. In reading newspapers, magazines, reports, contracts, correspondence; in listening to radio and television; in talking with others, and in every medium of verbal communication, you'll find yourself consciously processing information—discriminating and discounting information according to the communication efficiency of the writers and speakers. And doing that will help you to express your own ideas more efficiently.

A Memory Jogger

If you need help to recall the names of the seven principles, here is a little trick that should help. Notice that the initial letters of the principles are P-A-P-A-F-Q-C. You can remember them in that order by adapting the initials to a nonsense statement like *P*eter *A*nd *P*aul *A*re *F*rightening *Q*uiet *C*onnie.

Finally, it may help you to enlist the cooperation of an associate, correspondent, or friend—or your spouse or secretary if you have one. Explain your purpose and ask for honest criticism. If your confederate shares your interest in efficient communication, try to make it a two-way operation. Either way, you will surely improve your own communication efficiency.

3

Boo-Boos, Bar-Bars, and No-Noes

"O wad some Pow'r the giftie gie us
To see oursels as others see us!
It wad frae mony a blunder free us,
And foolish notion."
— *Robert Burns (To A Louse)*

Sooner or later, if you seriously wish to communicate efficiently you probably will find yourself interested also in communicating correctly. In particular you'll become concerned for correct pronunciation, spelling, and usage.

But you may ask, What standard shall I honor? Who can guide me? Even the dictionaries disagree. Isn't correctness, after all, a shifting sand?

To answer the last question first, no. Correctness is no shifting sand. It lacks the rigidity of Gibraltar, to be sure; but it distorts very slowly. Correctness is more like malleable metal, yielding but cohesive and unmercurial. It responds to sustained preference among the educated, but its change is never hurried by the pressure of vulgarity.

Shall we define vulgarity? The word vulgarity is derived from a Latin word meaning "of the mob or common people." The implication is plain: vulgar means common or second-rate, and vulgarity means coarseness as opposed to refinement—tastelessness as opposed to taste. And taste? Taste—good taste, that is—is the ability to distinguish and the inclination to prefer what is esthetically superior.

But I'm digressing.

What Is Correctness?

Our word *correct* is derived from a Latin verb meaning "to lead straight." For this context the dictionary definition of correct is "freedom from fault or error as judged by some standard." In turn, our word *standard* comes from Germanic and Old English verbs meaning "to stand." Its relevant dictionary definition is "any definite rule, principle, or measure established by authority."

Thus, we can say that correctness means freedom from fault or error as judged by the standard of respected authoritative practice. But who shall designate such practice? And can we hope for agreement where grammarians and lexicographers bicker? Probably not. So let's forget about unison and keep our eyes on correctness.

Correct standard English now embraces scores, maybe hundreds, of optional pronunciations, spellings, and usages: elections like saying *EE-ther* or *EYE-ther*, spelling counselor with one or two *l*'s, and using *lend* and *loan* interchangeably. Our culture has demanded such options, and they have gradually achieved correctness.

With so many options it seems fair to ask, isn't it sometimes hard to tell what is truly correct?

Yes, correctness is sometimes hard to find. Whom can you trust? Who or what should be our model? Probably least reliable, as a class, are the popular heroes of our times—the people you encounter in the newspapers or on the stage, screen, radio, television talk shows— people who "surely ought to know." Often the most flagrant and indefensible errors are committed by famous and supposedly educated men or women. For example, I seldom hear the word "schism" pronounced correctly by anyone who writes "Ph.D." after his name. But the unawareness of the multitides is little comfort to the sensitive.

Geeks and Greeks

Cultivated people who cherish their mother tongue are often sharply resentful of its abuse. You may remember the scene in Gilbert and Sullivan's comic operetta, *H.M.S. Pinafore*, where Captain Corcoran admonishes his daughter Josephine to consider the consequences of her budding romance with Ralph Rakstraw, "a common sailor." Shuddering for the embarrassment that young Rakstraw's untutored speech would invite, the old captain solemnly cautions Josephine, " . . . at every step he would surely commit solecisms that society would never pardon." The scene's hilarity in no way discredits the captain's observation.

To avoid presuming, let me consider the possibility that you are unacquainted with that word solecism, which is pronounced *SAHL-eh-sizzem*. The British anglicized it from a Latin word that the Romans had appropriated from the Greeks. To the Greeks, who coined it, the word *soloikos* meant "speaking incorrectly." I believe that is a charitable translation, because they used it disdainfully in referring to the people of Soloi, in ancient Cilicia, who spoke a corrupt Attic dialect which the cultivated Greeks regarded as near-barbarian. Our English word solecism now means any incorrectness in speech or writing.

The word barbarian has an interesting history of its own, also traceable to Greek speech sensitivity. Long before the birth of Christ, Athenians expressed their contempt for the rude babbling of uncultivated immigrants from other lands, designating their speech "bar-bar," probably in imitation of the way it sounded. Even today, linguists are sometimes tempted to dismiss certain rustic tongues as bar-bar, and we speak of particularly coarse or ugly solecisms as bar-bars.

The Great Debauch

So much for history. Unfortunately for modern English, today's Americans are more forgiving than yesterday's Greeks. Corrupting our language has become almost a national pastime, a game for everyone to enjoy. In every popular medium, and increasingly in our universities, we Americans seem to delight in subtle and outrageous perversions of standard English pronunciation, spelling, and usage.

"Language was made for man, not man for language!" runs the prevailing thought; "Let's make what we like of it." Liberal lexicographers promote such debauchery by tacitly implying that normality and vulgarity are essentially the same. (The editors of *Webster's Third New International Dictionary*[3] hesitate to discriminate clearly

3. G. & C. Merriam Company, Springfield, Massachusetts.

between standard and nonstandard English, piously maintaining that a dictionary should describe what people are saying, not prescribe what they ought to be saying.)

Yet normality and vulgarity are fundamentally different, as they must be. Normality must show what is correct whether it is popular or unpopular. What is normal must be legitimate; and legitimacy must reflect something nobler than mere plurality. An atrocity remains an atrocity no matter how many people commit it, and regardless of their attitudes in doing so.

Thus, if thousands of educated Americans suddenly began saying "he don't," it would still take an uncertain number of years before "he don't" superseded or gained equality with "he doesn't" as standard English. It probably would be several decades. Liberal scholars might welcome it within a few months, but people of taste would disdain it for years, and with sound reason.

Why? We have, and it is no happenstance, a traditional discipline in our language. Probably no one really loves the word "grammar," even grammarians; but surely the ordered structure of our language benefits all of us. Solomon laid down a fine principle when he wrote, "Remove not the ancient landmark that your fathers have set" (Proverbs 22: 28). Men of wisdom and taste have heeded that teaching in all the arts.

Let the debauch proceed, then. But let us give it no help.

Who Has the Stick?

To return to our earlier question: What is respected authoritative practice? Where can we find it? Who holds a reliable standard? If we can't trust the nearest dictionary, newscaster, columnist, politician, or celebrity, where shall we turn for guidance?

In the qualities discussed in this chapter—pronunciation, spelling, and usage—probably the most convenient and generally helpful ready reference authority is a conservative English dictionary, the more comprehensive the better (see chapter 5). But you should learn to use it fully, not merely to verify spellings and confirm what you think about the meanings of words, but also to broaden your understanding of your language and its derivations.

Get acquainted with your dictionary. Take the time to read its front matter, and learn your way around in its reference sections. Become familiar with its symbols for pronunciation and stressing of syllables. Read its "explanatory notes," which will dispel many mysteries regarding the parts of speech, inflectional forms, cross-references, capitalization, and other matters both interesting and important. In particular, learn your dictionary's common abbreviations; look individual ones up when you're in doubt.

If you feel that you need help in understanding your dictionary, swallow your pride and consult the nearest professional librarian. Possibly your city librarian will be most convenient. Any librarian should be proud to help you—and willing. Or inquire of a professional editor or English teacher, if you know one. The dictionary will be your servant as soon as you master it. Start now.

Besides a good dictionary, which you should own, there are other helpful books that you can borrow from libraries or use at their reference tables if you prefer not to buy them. However, I strongly recommend that you own several of the reference books discussed in chapter 5, particularly books on English usage and style.

Also, if you wish to pursue correctness in your own speech and writing, you should watch closely for the errors that others make, as well as those that you have been making. Listen for them on radio and television, in the meetings you attend, and wherever others speak. Be alert for them in your newspaper; most newspapers are riddled with errors in spelling and usage. Become sensitive to them in the magazines you read and the letters you receive. When you hear or read something of questionable correctness, check it immediately or as soon thereafter as you can.

If you're lucky enough to have a friend or associate who shares your interest in verbal correctness, perhaps you can agree to correct each other without injuring your relationship. But correctness is a prize to win, a privilege to enjoy graciously, not a burden to thrust upon others.

Pitfalls and Pratfalls

Following these few paragraphs I have listed more than a hundred of the most common blunders in contemporary American speech and writing. Each entry is coded P, S, or U, indicating the nature of the hazard as pronunciation, spelling, or usage. The list is obviously representative, nothing more. An exhaustive list of popular American solecisms would fill a large volume. But browse through it; you will surely find something of interest or controversy.

In the matter of pronunciation, in most instances I have indicated only one correct model, though I know that various dictionaries recognize alternate pronunciations for many if not most words of two or more syllables. The indicated pronunciation is always one that reflects settled conservative practice—practice that you can follow securely in the company of the correct. Practice the alternatives with caution.

For Latin words and phrases I have favored the pronunciations of New Latin, also called Late Latin, which is Latin as used since the medieval period, especially in scientific description and classification. Many of the vowel sounds differ greatly from those of classical Latin, including Catholic liturgical Latin. However, the New Latin pronunciations are generally consistent, convenient, reputable, and correct. The use of others is always questionable.

Possibly the makeshift means I have chosen to indicate pronunciation deserves an explanation. I have indicated sounds by combinations of vowels and consonants that are common, with equivalent sounds, in standard English; and I have indicated primary stressing with uppercase letters. It is obviously an imprecise method, but I think it serves its purpose adequately. It obviates the need for a system of diacritical marks which might more impede than help the instruction offered in a book of this kind.

Purposely omitted from the list that follows are many matters of usage too complex to be treated briefly. Some are matters of idiom; some are matters of grammar. Some are discussed in the following chapter, where readers who have little interest in such things can conveniently disregard them.

Now here are your boo-boos, bar-bars, and no-noes— the shibboleths of culture. And a shibboleth, in case you didn't know, is a kind of test; it's explained in the Old Testament in Judges chapter 12.

ABSENT (P)

Unlike the adjective, the verb—meaning to keep (one-

self) away—is stressed on the second syllable: *ab-SENT.*
Stress the second syllable in the verb's inflected forms also
—*ab-SENT-ed, ab-SENT-ing,* etc.

ACCESS, ACCESSIBLE, ACCESSORY (P)

That first *c* is sounded like a *k*, not like an *s.* Say *ACK-sess, ack-SESS-ib'l,* and *ack-SESS-ory.*

ACCLIMATE, ACCLIMATED (P)

Stress the second syllable in all forms of this verb: *ack-CLY-mat, ack-CLY-mat-ed,* etc.

A.D. (U)

Unlike B.C., A.D. should precede the year to which it
applies, e.g., A.D. 200 (not 200 A.D.). Since A.D. means
"in the year of our Lord," it is incorrect to say "the sixth
century A.D." Instead, just say "the sixth century."

ADDRESS (P)

Stress the second syllable in all forms of both the noun
and the verb: *ad-DRESS, ad-DRESSED, ad-DRESS-ing,*
etc.

AFFECT/EFFECT (S, U)

Affect can be either a noun or a verb; but as a noun it has
no use outside the technical jargon of psychology. As a
verb it means to impinge upon, influence, or sway; or to
pretend, feign, or assume an appearance of. We affect the
course of history by the way we vote; but we should never
affect holiness.

Effect, also, can be either a noun or a verb. As a noun
it means outcome, consequence, or result. As a verb it
means to make, produce, or accomplish. The effect of
tyranny is rebellion; and we can effect chaos by anarchy.

ALLS (P, S, U)

No matter where you find it, this quasi-plural word
alls, as in "Alls he said was . . . ," is illegitimate. Suppress the *s.*

AMENABLE, AMENABLY (P)
Say *am-EEN-ab'l* and *am-EEN-ab-lee.*

AMPHITHEATER (P)
Sound the *ph* like *f,* not *p.*

ANTE/ANTI (P, S, U)
Ante, which rhymes with *shanty,* means before. *Anti,* which rhymes with *can't I,* means opposed to. Sound them distinctly.

A POSTERIORI (P)
Say *ay post-eerie-OR-eye* (Latin, from the latter).

APOSTROPHE (S, U)
Use no apostrophe (') before the *s* in the possessive pronouns yours, ours, hers, its, and theirs; or in plurals like The Willoughbys. The apostrophe is correct in most other possessives, like Mr. Willoughby's rifle, the Willoughbys' summer home, at my wit's end, etc.; and in contractions like it's (it is), that's (that is), don't (do not), etc. Constructions that are more descriptive than possessive need no apostrophe, as in The Smothers Brothers Show.

APPENDIX (U)
The one you can lose surgically is singular—you have only one vermiform appendix. Therefore, the correct pronoun for it is *it,* not *them.*

APPLICABLE (P)
Say *AP-plick-ab'l,* not *ap-PLICK-ab'l*; and *in-AP-plick-ab'l,* not *in-ap-PLICK-ab'l.*

APPRAISE/APPRISE (P, S, U)
Appraise—the second syllable rhymes with *prays*—means to evaluate. *Apprise*—the second syllable rhymes with *prize*—means to inform.

A PRIORI (P)
Say *ay-pry-OR-eye* (Latin, from the former).

ASSURE/ENSURE/INSURE (P, S, U)

Assure means to give confidence to (someone). *Ensure* means to make certain. *Insure* means to protect or secure against injury or loss, as by casualty insurance. (I want to assure you that I have done everything possible to ensure that your jewels will be insured at their full market value.)

ATTORNEY/LAWYER (U)

An *attorney* is one who is authorized to transact business for another; he may or may not be a lawyer. A *lawyer* is one who is licensed to practice law; he may or may not be someone's attorney. Neither designation carries more dignity or respect than the other.

AYE (P, U)

As an adverb meaning yes, or a noun meaning an affirmative vote, aye is pronounced like the pronoun *I*. As an adverb meaning ever, always, or continually (usually in a poetic sense), aye is pronounced like the article *a*.

BEHALF (U)

In behalf of means for the benefit of (someone or something), as a friend or advocate. *On behalf of* means representing (a person, persons, or organization), as an agent or spokesman.

BEHEMOTH (P)

Say *BEE-em-awth*, not *bee-HEE-muth* or *bee-HEM-uth*.

BONA FIDE (P)

Fide rhymes with tidy.

BREAKFASTS (P)

Say *BRECK-fasts*, not *BRECK-fastez*.

CHAISE LONGUE (P, S)

Say *shezz LONG*. Pronounce the plural, chaises longues, the same way—*sheez LONG*. It's a French phrase meaning long chair, not lounge chair. Watch the spelling.

CHARISMA (U)

Charisma has only one correct secular meaning: a magnetic personal quality that enables certain individuals to command the loyalty of others. Thus, charisma cannot properly be attributed to animals, products, advertising, or ideas.

CHIROPODIST (P)

Say *ky-ROP-o-dist*. Sound the *ch* like *k*, the same as in chiropractor; but stress the second syllable.

COHORT (U)

A cohort is a military or other division, company, band, or group, not a colleague or associate.

COMPARABLE (P)

Say *COM-par-ab'l*. Stress the first syllable.

COMPLECTED (U)

Complected is illegitimate. The correct word is complexioned.

COMPLEMENTARY/COMPLIMENTARY (P, S, U)

Complementary means serving to fulfill, complete, or augment; its second syllable rhymes with hem. *Complimentary* means expressing or containing admiration, esteem, or respect; or gratuitous, i.e., free of charge. Its second syllable rhymes with him. In both words, stress the third syllable.

COMPOSE/COMPRISE (U)

Compose means to form, constitute, or create. *Comprise* means to embrace, include, or contain. The parts compose the whole; the whole comprises the parts. "Comprised of" is an illegitimate phrase.

COMPTROLLER (P)

Comptroller is pronounced exactly the same as *controller*.

CONSENSUS (S, U)

Consensus means general agreement or collective opinion; thus, the phrase "consensus of opinion" is redundant. Regarding spelling, note that the words consensus and census are unrelated.

CONSUMMATE (adjective) (P)

Stress the second syllable—say *con-SUM-at.*

CONTRACTUAL (P, S)

Contractual contains only one *r.* Pronounce and spell it accordingly.

CONTUMELY (P)

Stress the first syllablc and run the rest together—*CON-toom-elly.*

CONVINCE/PERSUADE (U)

Convince means to bring to belief or assent. *Persuade* means to induce or entice, with an implied emotional appeal. You can convince people of your honesty, but you must persuade them to buy your products. (You don't convince people to do something; you persuade them to do it.)

COST SAVING (U)

This is grammatically absurd. Costs may be reduced, not saved. Say *cost reduction.*

COUPON (P)

Say *COO-pon,* not *KYOO-pon.*

COVETOUS, COVETOUSNESS (P)

The second syllable is *et,* not *etch.*

CREDENCE (P)

Say *CREED-ence,* not *CRED-ence.*

CRITERIA, CRITERION (U)

Criteria is the plural of *criterion.* Use appropriate plural or singular articles, pronouns, and verb forms. (Criteria *are,* a criterion *is.*)

CURRENTLY/PRESENTLY (U)

Currently means now—at present. *Presently* means very soon—imminently.

DAIS (P, S, U) Also see LECTERN, PODIUM, and ROSTRUM

A dais (say *DAY-iss*) is a platform used to give prominence to an orchestra, head table, or speaker. It means the same thing as podium.

DESPICABLE, DESPICABLY (P)

Stress the first syllable—say *DESS-pick-ab'l* and *DESS-pick-ab-lee*.

DESULTORY (P)

Stress the first syllable—say *DESS-ull-tory*.

DILETTANTE (P, S, U)

Say *dill-eh-TANTY*, to rhyme with shanty (it's Italian); and watch the spelling. It means a person who loves the arts, or (with no implied disapproval) one who pursues an art or science superficially or sporadically.

DIPHTHERIA (P, S)

Stress the second syllable—say *dif-THEER-ee-ah*; and notice that the first syllable rhymes with riff, not rip.

DISSECT (P)

The first syllable is *dis*, not *die*.

DOUR (P, U)

Dour is a Scottish word that rhymes with poor, not power. It means gloomy, sullen, stern, or severe in expression.

DRAMATIS PERSONAE (P)

Stress the first syllable in *dramatis* and the second syllable in *personae*. Say *DRAM-at-iss per-SO-knee*.

DRAPERIES/DRAPES (U)

Draperies are fabric panels hung in folds for decoration or privacy. *Drapes* is a substandard synonym for draperies.

EFFECT See AFFECT/EFFECT

E.G. (U) Also see I.E. and VIZ.

E.g. is the abbreviation for *exempli gratia* (Latin, for example). It does not mean "that is" or "namely," thus it is not synonymous with *i.e.* or *viz.*

ENSURE See ASSURE/ENSURE/INSURE

ENVELOP/ENVELOPE (P, S, U)

Envelop, a verb, means to enclose or enfold; stress the second syllable—say *en-VELL-op*. *Envelope*, a noun, means a covering or wrapper, usually of paper; stress the first syllable and pronounce it *EN-vell-ope* (the first syllable rhymes with hen).

EPITOME (U)

An epitome is a representative digest, condensation, or portion, not a quintessence, model, or archetype.

ERRATA (P)

Say *air-ATE-ah*, not *air-AT-ah* or *air-AHT-ah*.

ET AL. (P, U)

Et al. is the abbreviation for *et alii* (Latin, and others). The abbreviation should be read as if spelled out—*et ALE-ee-eye*, or simply *et ALE*.

ET CETERA (P)   Also see ETC. in chapter 4

The first syllable is pronounced *et*, not *ek*.

EVIDENTLY (P)

Stress the first styllable—say *EV-id-ent-ly*, not *ev-id-ENT-ly*.

EXPLICABLE/INEXPLICABLE (P)

Stress the first syllable—say *EX-plick-ab'l*, not *ex-PLICK-ab'l*; and *in-EX-plick-ab'l*, not *in-ex-PLICK-ab'l*. (If that's too difficult, say explainable and unexplainable.

FARTHER/FURTHER (comparative adjectives) (U)

Farther means more distant physically; *further* means more distant in some other way. (Pleasantville is farther from Schenectady than it is from Albany. But world peace may be further away than we hope.)

FIANCÉ/FIANCÉE (P, S, U)

Fiancé is masculine; fiancée is feminine. They're pronounced the same. Stress the last syllable—*fee-ahn-SAY*.

FINIS (P, U)

Finis (Latin, end or conclusion) is pronounced *FINE-iss*.

FLAUNT/FLOUT (U)

Flaunt means to display ostentatiously. *Flout* means to treat contemptuously. (Bandits flaunt their weapons and flout the law.)

FORTE (P, U)

Forte, meaning one's strong point, is pronounced *FORT*. *Forte*, meaning loudly or powerfully, or a musical passage to be played that way, is pronounced *FOR-tay*.

FORTUITOUS (U)

Fortuitous means occurring by chance or accident. It is no synonym for fortunate.

FOYER (P)

Foyer rhymes with employer.

GANTLET/GAUNTLET (P, S, U)

Pronounce both *GAWNT-let*. *Gantlet* means a kind of punishment—"running the gantlet." *Gauntlet* means a protective glove worn by knights. Throwing a gauntlet to the ground implied a challenge; figuratively, gauntlet means challenge.

GESTURE/GESTICULATE (P)

The first syllable rhymes with jest, not guest.

GRATIS (P)

Say *GRATE-iss* (Latin, without charge).

GRIMACE (P)

Stress the second syllable—say *grim-ACE*.

GYNECOLOGIST, GYNECOLOGY (P)

The *gyn* rhymes with gin, the same as it does in the other Greek-rooted words misogynist, philogynist, and polygynist.

HANGED/HUNG (U)

Hanged means executed by hanging, usually as a criminal sentence. *Hung* means suspended, deadlocked, or draped.

HARA-KIRI (P, S, U)

Hara-kiri, note the spelling, is pronounced *Hah-rah KEER-ee*. It means ritual suicide. However, the Japanese prefer the more ceremonious term *seppuku* (say seh-POO-koo).

HARASS (P)

In all the inflections of this verb stress the *first* styllable: *HAR-ass*, *HAR-ass-ing*, *HAR-ast*, *HAR-ass-ment*, etc.

HEALTHFUL/HEALTHY (U)

Healthful means conducive to health. *Healthy* means having health. Vitamins may be healthful; people who take vitamins may become healthy.

HEIGHT (P)

Height ends with a hard *t* sound, not a soft *th* sound.

HEINOUS (P, U)

Say *HAY-in-us*. It means hatefully or shockingly evil.

HOME/HOUSE (U)

A *home* is a family abode; the thought is more sentimental than tangible. You can make your home in a house, apartment, condominium, igloo, or almost anywhere. A *house* is a structure for creature habitation; it is of course tangible. You can build, buy, sell, or trade houses, not homes. (The hucksterish coinage *townhome* is unwelcome among the cultivated.)

HOPEFULLY (U)

Hopefully means in a hopeful manner, just as carefully means in a careful manner. To use hopefully as if it means "I hope that" or "it is to be hoped that" is incorrect, no matter who uses it that way.

HOSPITABLE (P)

Stress the first syllable—*HOSP-it-ab'l*, not *hosp-IT-ab'l.*

I.E. (U) Also see E.G. and VIZ.

I.e. is the abbreviation for *id est* (Latin, that is). It does not mean "for example" or "namely," thus it is not synonymous with *e.g.* or *viz.*

ILK (U)

A Scottish word, ilk means "of the same name or place." It is nonsynonymous with kind or sort.

IMPIOUS (P)

Stress the first syllable—*IMP-ee-us.* If you must stress the second syllable, say unpious, which means the same thing.

IMPLY/INFER (U)

Imply means to say indirectly—to hint or suggest. *Infer* means to deduce. Writers and speakers imply; readers and listeners infer.

INCIDENCE/INCIDENT (P, S, U)

Disregarding its scientific meanings, *incidence* means an act, fact, or manner of falling upon or affecting; or a range of occurrence or influence. *Incident* means an event or occurrence, often a minor one.

INCOGNITO (P, U)

Stress the second syllable—*in-COG-nit-oh.* It means under an unknown or unrecognizable name, with one's true identity concealed.

INEXPLICABLE See EXPLICABLE/INEXPLICABLE

INEXTRICABLE, INEXTRICABLY (P)

Stress the second syllable—*in-EX-trick-ab'l, in-EX-trick-ab-lee.*

INFER See IMPLY/INFER
INSURE See ASSURE/ENSURE/INSURE
INTRODUCE (P)

The second syllable rhymes with crow, not cur; sound it clearly. Never say *inter-DOOCE.*

IRREVOCABLE, IRREVOCABLY (P)

Stress the second syllable—*ear-REV-oke-ab'l* and *ear-REV-oke-ab-ly,* not *ear-rev-OKE-ab'l* and *ear-rev-OKE-ab-ly.*

ITALIAN (P)

The first syllable rhymes with bit, not bite.

LACKADAISICAL (P, S)

Note that the first syllable is lack, not lax.

LARGESS or LARGESSE (P)

Stress the first syllable—*LARGE-ess.*

LARYNX (P, S)

Say *LAR-inks,* not *LAR-nicks*; and watch the spelling.

LAWYER See ATTORNEY/LAWYER
LAY/LIE (U)

With few exceptions, *lay* is a transitive verb and *lie* is an intransitive verb. (The only way you can lay down is to deposit feathers.)

LECTERN (U) Also see DAIS, PODIUM, and ROSTRUM

A lectern is a stand to hold a speaker's notes. It may stand on a table, on the floor, or on a dais, podium, or rostrum.

LIABLE/LIKELY (U)

Liable means obligated, responsible, susceptible, open, exposed, subject, or prone. You will be liable to censure if you use it as a synonym for *likely.*

LIVID (U)

Livid means black, blue, or ashen, not red or pink.

LONG-LIVED/SHORT-LIVED (P)

The lived rhymes with dived.

LOOSE/LOSE (P, S, U)

Loose (rhymes with noose) is an adjective meaning slack, or a verb meaning to release. *Lose* (rhymes with booze) is a verb meaning to be deprived of, or to forfeit. You *lose* (not loose) sleep, money, or face.

MACHINATION (P)

The first syllable rhymes with back, not bash.

MISCHIEVOUS (P)

Say *MISS-chee-vuss*, not *miss-CHEE-vee-uss*.

MOTION/MOVE (U)

Say, "Mr. Chairman, I *move* that . . . ," not " . . . make a *motion* that . . . "

NAUSEATED/NAUSEOUS (U)

Nauseated means sick at the stomach, or deeply disgusted. *Nauseous* means sickening, or tending to cause nausea.

NÉE (P, U)

It rhymes with hay, and means born. Therefore, it can only apply to one's family name, not one's given name. In American usage the accent mark is optional.

NUCLEAR/NUCLEUS (P, S)

Say *NOO-klee-ar* and *NOO-klee-us*, not *NOO-kyoo-lar* and *NOO-kyoo-luss*.

ORGY (P)

Rhymes with Georgie, not Porgy.

ORIENT/ORIENTATE (P, S, U)

The correct word is *orient*. *Orientate* is illegitimate.

PATINA (P)

Stress the first syllable—*PAT-in-ah*, not *pa-TEEN-ah*.

PERCOLATE, PERCOLATOR (P, S, U)

Say *PERK-uh-late*, not *PERK-yuh-late*, etc. It means to seep through, not boil or bubble.

PER SE (P, U)

Say *per SEE* (Latin, by or in itself; intrinsically).

PERSONA NON GRATA (P)

Say *per-SOAN-ah non GRATE-ah* (Latin, an unacceptable, unwelcome, or objectionable person).

PERSUADE See CONVINCE/PERSUADE

PHENOMENA, PHENOMENON (S, U)

Phenomena is the plural of *phenomenon*. Use appropriate plural or singular articles, pronouns, and verb forms. (Phenomena *are*, a phenomenon *is*.)

PLENARY (P, U)

Rhymes with beanery, not hennery. It means full or complete.

PODIATRIST (P)

Stress the second styllable—*po-DIE-ah-tryst*.

PODIUM (U) Also see DAIS, LECTERN, and ROSTRUM

A podium is a platform used to give prominence to an orchestra, head table, or speaker. It means the same thing as dais.

PORE/POUR (S, U)

Pore means to read studiously or attentively, or to ponder; it is usually followed by the preposition *over*. *Pour* means to flow in a stream.

PRECEDENCE (P, S, U)

Stress the second syllable—*pre-SEED-ence*. It means priority or preference of place, privilege, honor, or authority.

PRECEDENT (S) (P, S, U)

As an *adjective*, precedent (stress the second syllable

—*pre-SEED-ent*) means prior in place, privilege, honor, or authority. As a *noun*, precedent (stress the first syllable —*PRESS-eh-dent*) means an earlier occurrence of something similar or analogous; its plural, precedents, is stressed the same way as the singular form.

PRESENTLY See CURRENTLY/PRESENTLY

PREVENTATIVE/PREVENTIVE (P, S)

Preventive is correct. *Preventative* is illegitimate.

QUASI (P, U)

Say *KWAY-sigh*, to rhyme with mayfly. (Latin, as if.)

REALTOR (P, U)

Say *REE-al-tor*, not *REEL-ah-tor*. A realtor is a real estate broker who is a member of the National Association of Realtors. Not all real estate agents are realtors.

RELATIONS/RELATIVES (U)

Relations are acts or associations. *Relatives* are kinsfolk. To confuse them can be embarrassing.

REMUNERATION (P)

Sound the second syllable like *myoon*, not *noom*.

RENEGE (P, S)

Say *re-NIG* or *re-NEG*, and watch the spelling.

REVEREND, REV. (U)

The popular blunder is to call a Protestant clergyman *Rev. Smith*, as if reverend were a name of rank like captain or mayor. Actually, reverend is a title of respect, like honorable; you'd never think of calling Senator Kennedy "Hon. Kennedy."

So, the title reverend should always be used with its holder's given name or initials, in addition to his surname. Obviously, there is no such thing as "a reverend."

Properly, we should address a Protestant clergyman as Mr. Smith (or in some situations, Pastor Smith) unless we know it is appropriate to call him Dr. Smith, or unless we know him well enough to call him by his given name.

In formal writing we should spell out The Reverend or The Right Reverend, as appropriate (or the abbreviation The Rev. or The Rt. Rev.), followed by his full name as he uses it customarily. In less formal writing The may be omitted, but Rev. should always be followed by both given name and surname. Or you can say the Rev. Mr. Smith.

Catholic usage is more complex but seems to present fewer problems. For further guidance consult one of the authorities on etiquette.

REVOCABLE (P)

Stress the first syllable—*REV-oke-ab'l*, not *rev-OKE-ab'l*.

ROSTRUM (U) Also see DAIS, LECTERN, and PODIUM

A rostrum is a stage for public speaking, or a raised platform for that purpose. Thus, a rostrum is a kind of dais or podium.

SAVING/SAVINGS (U)

You can make worthwhile *savings* by smart shopping; but not *a* worthwhile savings. Use the singular noun with the singular article: a worthwhile *saving*.

SCHISM (P)

Say *SIZZ-em*, not *SHIZZ-em* or *SKIZZ-em*.

SEPULCHRE (P)

Say *SEP-ul-ker*, not *SEP-luh-ker*.

SHORT-LIVED See LONG-LIVED/SHORT-LIVED
SUBJECT (P)

As a verb, stress the second syllable—*sub-JECT*. Also, *sub-JECT-ed*, *sub-JECT-ing*, etc.

SUBSIDIARY (P, S)

Say *sub-SID-ee-airy*, not *sub-SID-er-airy*.

VAGARY, VAGARIES (P)

Stress the second syllable—*va-GAIR-ee, va-GAIR-eez.*

VALANCE/VALENCE (P, S, U)

A *valance* (say *VAL-ance*) is a kind of short drapery or drapery heading. A *valence* (say *VAIL-ence*) is a chemical degree or unit of combining power, or a relative capacity to unite, react, or interact.

VIS-À-VIS (P, U)

Stress the final syllable—say *veez-ah-VEE.* As a preposition it means face-to-face with, compared with, or confronted with. As an adverb it means in company, or together. As a noun it means an opposite number or partner; the plural is spelled the same but pronounced *veez-ah-VEEZ.*

VIZ. (P, U) Also see E.G. and I.E.

Viz. is the abbreviation for *videlicet* (Latin, that is to say, or namely), pronounced *vid-ELL-iss-et.* In reading aloud, pronounce the abbreviation to rhyme with fizz.

YE (P, U)

As a personal pronoun meaning you, ye is pronounced *yee.* As an archaic article meaning the, ye is pronounced as if it were spelled t-h-e—*the.*

4

Facility and Felicity— Grammar, Idiom, and Style

"A word fitly spoken is like apples of gold
in a setting of silver."
—*Solomon (Proverbs 25: 11, RSV)*

We have talked at length about efficiency and correctness. We come logically to the province of grammar, idiom, and style.

Maybe we should begin by defining our terms. *Grammar* is a branch of the science of philology, or linguistics, that deals with a language's inflections, phonetic system, and syntax. Most of us got a smattering of grammar in grade school; and most of us hated it—at least, we learned to say that we did. Its teachers inflicted on us the drudgeries of words and their classifications, purposes, tenses, moods, and such things, and forced us to diagram sentences showing word and thought relationships.

Idiom is a customary manner of expression. For you

and me it is the customary manner of verbal expression among English-speaking Americans, i.e., literate Americans generally. Unlike grammar, idiom is totally unscientific. It follows no rules or principles at all, just popular assent. When grammar and idiom conflict, as they often do, idiom tends to prevail in all but the most formal circumstances, and sometimes even there. So, what is correct is not always grammatical. For example, contrary to grammar, it is idiomatic to say "It's me."

Style is a manner of expressing thought in language. Thus, there are King James style, Edwardian style, legal style, medical style, lyric poetry style, *Time* magazine style, and many others. And authors sometimes develop recognizable styles of their own—for example, Balzac, de Maupassant, Faulkner, Wolfe, Conrad, and Doyle.

Effective style usually reflects not only imagination but also some grasp of grammar and idiom. You must be very long on imagination to compensate for shortness in grammar and idiom, and very long on both idiom and imagination to compensate for serious defects in grammar. But none of us is perfect, and few approach literary distinction. However, to the degree that you seek proficiency as a writer or speaker you must develop a disciplined respect for grammar and idiom—and you should try to develop a consistent style of expression.

Gateway to the Straight Way

If you are old enough to be reading this book you have probably learned as much formal grammar as you will ever know. You are unlikely ever to return to declining pronouns, parsing verbs, and diagraming sentences. And if you have been saying things like "between he and I" since you were a child, you probably will say them always.

Beyond efficiency and correctness, then, your improvement area is pretty clearly centered on idiom and style. You can do much to improve your mastery of idiom, and develop a lucid and pleasing style of expression, by emulating the practice of worthy writers and speakers.

Of everything I have ever read about idiom, the most stimulating and generally helpful counsel I have found is *The Careful Writer*,[4] by Theodore M. Bernstein, a newspaperman. However, you can begin with advantage by reading E. B. White's witty and penetrating observations in the chapter titled "An Approach to Style" in *The Elements of Style*,[5] a book whose central contents were written by William Strunk, Jr. You'll read more about both of these books in chapter 5.

Before proceeding, I would like to tell you a few of Mr. White's comments. He says, "Writing is, for most, laborious and slow. The mind travels faster than the pen; consequently, writing becomes a question of learning to make occasional wing shots, bringing down the bird of thought as it flashes by." Most helpfully, he says, " . . . to achieve style, begin by affecting none—that is, place yourself in the background." He counsels also, and I heartily agree, that basic to good style is the matter of "ear"—learning to sense intuitively what sounds right and plausible, which demands consistent attention to what capable speakers and writers are saying, and how they are saying it.

Your goal, then, beyond having something worthwhile to say, is to learn to say it tellingly, correctly, and felici-

---

4. Atheneum, New York, 1965.
5. Macmillan, New York, 1959.

tously. And that is an art that requires aptitude, study, and practice, practice, practice. If your work involves verbal communication beyond casual conversation—as it does if you prepare correspondence, instructions, or reports—you can practice much of your basic communication skill on company time, to your and your employer's common advantage.

The Sociable Approach

Either way, you can benefit greatly by associating with others who share your interest in verbal communication, regardless of your field. Basic to the development of *oral* speech skill is to grow accustomed to the trappings and hazards of the formal speech situation—the lectern and all that goes with it. That and much more is available to you through any local chapter of Toastmasters International or International Toastmistress. Incidentally, Toastmasters is now coeducational. The cost of membership in such clubs is quite modest. The training they provide is priceless, and the social enjoyment alone is well worth the effort.

Among other things, as an active Toastmaster or Toastmistress you will quickly learn how to think on your feet, maintain a graceful posture, use gestures effectively, pitch your voice for greatest effectiveness, avoid nervousness, acknowledge an introduction, introduce other speakers correctly, and conclude your speech without awkwardness. Also, you will learn to conquer awkward pauses, use humor with good taste, and avoid the ugliest pitfalls of both reading speeches and delivering them extemporaneously.

Beyond Toastmasters or Toastmistress training you can get, if you really need it, either private coaching or classroom training in speech technique in most cities. And if you're sufficiently interested you can query speakers and teachers in other cities by mail. Good places to start inquiring in these areas are chambers of commerce, public libraries, adult education centers, and liberal arts colleges or junior colleges.

If your interest is in fiction, nonfiction, poetry, advertising, commercial journalism, or technical writing, there are other organizations that would welcome you into their membership whether you are a student, professional, or dilettante. To learn the names and addresses of those that would most interest you, inquire at your city library, college library, or local chamber of commerce. People who practice communication seek the company of others who are similarly inclined, and they will welcome your inquiry.

In fact, to pursue verbal communication in a social vacuum would be self-defeating. Communication is an art that demands practice, which can only be accomplished by imparting information frequently from one place to another, preferably among people of similar interests.

Selfishness in this matter would rob others, of course; but worst of all, it would rob you. Therefore, whatever your particular communication interest, you will further your own development by sharing it with others in appropriate social, fraternal, or professional exercises. Lawyers, physicians, theologians, and other professionals have been doing it for centuries; you should do it too.

Idiom and Style

Before going further I ask you to remember that, unlike grammar, idiom and style are essentially artistic, not sci-

entific. Grammar insists on certain things and forbids
others that idiom and style disregard. Idiom and style
heed no discipline but "ear"—the right sound of phrases
and usages that earn acceptance through general practice
within a nation's culture.

Idiom changes very slowly. And sometimes old idiom
is so appealing to the ear that it survives in parallel with
newer idiom. For example, the idiom of correct formal
English in the time of King James still sounds dignified,
stately, and beautiful to most of us, even though we no
longer customarily speak or write that way. To some of
us it's quite compelling, so that we tend to use the King
James idiom when we pray, although we would never use
it in writing a letter or a report.

The point to remember here is that popularity is not
the only parent of idiom. Idiom is the product of both
popularity (particularly among people of good taste and
cultural influence) and time. And style, in any age, involves the felicitous exercise of both idiom and grammar.
Now, here are a number of things to think about and watch
for if you wish to tread the safer paths in grammar, idiom,
and style:

A/AN

Use *a* preceding a consonant sound and *an* preceding a
vowel sound in both speech and writing. What counts is
the sound that follows the article, not the letter. So, just
as you'd say *a* merchant and *an* accountant, say *an* FHA
loan and *a* European custom. And write them the way
you'd say them: *a* N.Y. restaurant, for example.

And note this. The use of *an* preceding words that begin
with a sounded *h*, like history or Hellenist, is a literary

affectation that you'll do well to avoid.

CLICHÉS

On the outside chance that someone has forgotten, a cliché is a stale, hackneyed, overworked expression. Our language contains hundreds of them, and they tend to be addicting. Most of them lost their power to enrich communication decades ago, and now all they do is weary our eyes and ears. You should fight any tendency to practice them with the same resolve that an earnest alcoholic should fight his weakness for whiskey. If you let them, clichés will undermine your effectiveness as a verbal communicator.

Here are some representative clichés, none of which can possibly help you to communicate more efficiently, correctly, or gracefully:

> Six of one or half a dozen of the other
> By the same token
> Each and every one
> Few and far between
> Cute as a bug's ear
> I could (or couldn't) care less
> Whys and wherefores

Clichés reflect a kind of poisonous banality that will stifle the freshness and vigor that your thoughts might otherwise project. Force yourself to resist the inclination to use them; make yourself find nonstereotyped phrases to express your ideas, even if it slows you down for a while. Cultivate your taste for fresh, untainted expression.

CUTENESS

Here is another archenemy of felicitous prose and good conversation—the deliberate injection of contrived cleverness or outrageous dialect that offends good taste. Here are a few illustrations.

From a patron's memo to a postmaster:
  "Prithee, sire, sequester my missives till I
  return from my hegira to the great City."
From a clerk's response to a telephone inquiry:
  "Speak up, daddy-o . . . "
From a chatterbox gossip column:
  "Frank Sinatra winged into town yesterday, inked
  a hush-hush contract, bunked at the Warwick, and
  flashed back to his swankienda in Palm Springs."

But no more; I'm beginning to gag. If cuteness needs a home, let it dwell outside the gate.

ETC.

The use of *etc.* to avoid focusing ideas clearly is a mark of greenness, laziness, or ineptness. It never fails to discount the speaker's or writer's merit in the eyes of the discerning, and is gruesomely unprofessional when it appears in an employment résumé, as in "Designed and debugged business control systems for inventory management, personnel records, cost analysis, etc." The best way to express that kind of idea is the "including" way, e.g., "Designed and debugged business control systems for major industrial requirements including inventory management, personnel records, and cost analysis."

The use of *etc.* is truly fitting only where what follows it is foreseeable or conjecturable, as in "Screw machine products such as threaded studs, cap screws, hex bolts, etc."

GOT

Got is the past participle of the verb infinitive *to get*. As such, it has many legitimate uses. But as an intensifier for the verb infinitive *to have*, *got* is an ugly and illegitimate word. If you have the habit of saying things like "I've got to go" and "We've got two cars," break the habit. Instead, say "I have to go," "I must go," or "I'm going"; and "We have two cars," or "We own two cars." The phrase "got to" is substandard English.

IF/WHETHER

If is becoming idiomatic as a substitute for *whether* in certain (but not all) sentence constructions; it even has Scriptural precedent (see Genesis 8:8, most classical translations). However, if the gist of your idea is "whether or not," say *whether*, not *if*; you'll be on safer ground.

ORTHODOXY

There may be times when you'll want to put an uncommon concept in words, as one technical writer did when he wrote, " . . . less than approximately 500 feet." It was valid in its context, as the editor learned when he talked with the author. But it deserved an explanation.

Another engineer startled an editor with this: "The errors due to uncertainty of location, radiometric differences, and digital quantized noise usually cannot be minimized altogether."

When you feel that you must express something in strange or strange-sounding language, consider the possibility that readers or listeners may miss your point. If there is any reasonable doubt, be kind enough to say "That is, . . . ," "In other words . . . ," or whatever it takes to explain.

PLURALOSIS

Whenever you see phrases like "sports coat," "good communications," "systems analysis," "a substantial savings," or "policies and procedures manual," you see evidence of literary superstition. Inappropriate pluralizing of nouns and adjectives usually betrays a false notion that pluralizing somehow intensifies a word's meaning, which of course it does not; it merely betrays the writer's or speaker's ineptness. (Would you take your car to an "automobiles garage" for a "cylinders reborings"?)

PREPOSITIONS

Prepositions are those supplemental words like *to, from, for, against,* and *of,* to name just a few of them, that introduce other words or phrases. Verb infinitives always take the preposition *to.* Prepositional phrases like "kicked *from* pillar *to* post," "*for* goodness' sake," *against* all odds," and "the roof *of* the house," are necessary to grammatical continuity and meaning.

Three prepositional abuses are particularly offensive to sensitive ears and eyes, and you should guard against them:

1. Never insert *of* between a modifier and the thing modified, as in "too nice of a day to stay indoors," or "too heavy of a burden for me to carry." Omit the *of.*

2. Never use *of* to elaborate the proposition *off,* as in "fell off of his chair," or "just off of the highway." Omit the *of.*

3. Avoid strings of prepositional phrases such as "the author of the stories about the adventures of the daughter of the foreman of the dude ranch." You can seldom truly justify more than two prepositional phrases in a single simple sentence, and many are easily eliminated by simply combining ideas. For example, the string quoted could be shortened to "the author of the adventure stories about the dude-ranch foreman's daughter."

PUNCTUATION (INCLUDING CAPITALIZATION)

If you take punctuation seriously, as you should, you will probably need a good style guide (see chapter 5). You should learn your way around in your style guide, and refer to it often. Meanwhile, you might well consider the following ideas.

The legitimate purpose of punctuation and capitalization is to help the reader. What facilitates reading, aids comprehension, precludes misunderstanding, or honors worthy tradition is good punctuation—or good capitalization. All other puncuation or capitalization is bad because it will tend to slow and possibly confuse or irritate the reader, maybe even mislead him. Here are several rules.

Commas. Use a comma wherever you would (or should) pause briefly in speaking a series of words, and nowhere else except where convention demands it, as between the names of cities and states, or in dates written in the form May 3, 1975. In every series of three or more words or phrases insert a comma after each one that precedes the terminal *and*, including especially the one that immediately precedes the *and*. Omitting that last comma can invite confusion. Newspaper writers and advertising copywriters often ignore this rule, but the rule stands on solid ground. Respect it.

Hyphens. Avoid hyphenating prefixes like *pre, post, ante, anti, supra, infra*, unless you're certain that omitting the hyphen would invite ambiguity. Usually it will not. The hyphen is offensive in constructions like co-operating, pre-eminent, re-reading, non-responsive etc., because it strikes the reader's eye with needless punctuation. Words like *fleabite, dockhand*, and *coldblooded* need no hyphen and should have none. For others you must use your head or consult a compounding guide or dictionary.

Capitalization. The risk of failing to capitalize a legitimately proper name or adjective is slight; most people overcapitalize. You needn't capitalize a.m., p.m., a.c., d.c., or other abbreviations for common words. And you needn't capitalize descriptive names, usually, unless they serve as official titles. Thus, although on a signature line you would write *John Brown, Manager*, in text you would write *John Brown, the manager.* Don't overcapitalize.

TELL vs DISTINGUISH

In informal speech and writing, *tell* is beginning to become idiomatic as equivalent to *distinguish*: "You can't tell the boys from the girls." However, wise conservative practice is slow to follow the trend. I say avoid it; if you mean distinguish, say distinguish, at least in formal writing.

THANK YOU

Here is a small but important matter of style you should know about when you address an assembly. You'd learn it quickly in a Toastmasters or Toastmistress club, but I realize you may never join one. Whether you're speaking extemporaneously or impromptu, or reading your speech, when you finish speaking just sit down. Don't say "Thank you."

Saying "Thank you" at the end of a speech is no mark of courtesy. Rather it's a mark of ignorance and a sign of weakness that you should avoid like a plague. The courtesy that you owe your audience is to say something meaningful and end of a high note of summary, emphasis, or exhortation. Make your concluding words meaningful; leave your audience with a clear, pointed idea to think about. Where you have time to prepare, rehearse your concluding statement word for word.

Ordinarily you owe your audience no thanks, and you may embarrass them by saying "Thank you." Instead, they owe you their attention or at least their respectful silence while you are speaking. If they like what you say they may thank *you*, probably by applauding. But don't thank them; it's bad form.

THAT/WHICH

The relative pronouns *that* and *which* have particular uses and are not always interchangeable. Neither is more literary or respectable than the other. Here is a little chart that may help you use them correctly:

	That	*Which*
Nature	Defining	Clarifying
Character	Restrictive	Nonrestrictive
Purpose	Limit or identify	Comment
Function	Essential	Parenthetical
Punctuation	None	Commas usually
Example	Honor that is	Honor, which is
	lightly held is	hard to earn, is
	easily lost.	easy to forfeit.

VULGARISMS

A vulgarism is a word or expression originated or used chiefly by illiterate persons; or a substandard usage; or a coarse word or phrase. That's what a popular dictionary says. Slang seems to rank a little higher, being "informal nonstandard English composed typically of coinages, arbitrarily changed words, and extravagant, forced, or facetious figures of speech."

Anyone can see that vulgarisms and slang have a lot in common, including their ancestry. They appeal mainly to those who lack confidence in their ability to express ideas in correct English, i.e., standard English; and to those whose purpose is to scorn "the establishment" and identify with what they fancy is a more liberated culture. I think we can apply the term vulgarisms to both.

For many years the vulgarisms for money have included *kale, cabbage, lettuce, green, mazuma,* and many other things. Now we have *bread.* Concurrently, our nation's lexicon of vulgarity has acquired such sophisticated slang as *hangup, uptight, ripoff, rap, gay, pigs, groovy, uppers, downers, pot, hey man, oh wow, out of sight,* and scores if not hundreds of others.

They're real, aren't they? They're honest! And gutsy! They express human feelings! Who can outlaw them?

Such drivel is very real, but it remains illegitimate, however well-intended it may be. The privilege to speak and write drivel belongs to everyone, but cultivated persons don't exercise it. Behave like a cultivated person, whether you are one or not, and you will communicate better.

WHO/WHOM, WHOEVER/WHOMEVER

Educated Americans all seem to know that *who* is subjective and *whom* is objective, but few seem to understand the grammatical distinction. Here is a trick that may help you, as it sometimes does me.

Consider *who* and *whom* analogous to *he* and *him,* respectively; then see whether *he* or *him* would sound better, and be guided accordingly. (If you feel comfortable saying things like "She invited he and I," this will give you no help.)

You'll find a lucid explanation of the grammatical rule in any of Theodore M. Bernstein's books mentioned in chapter 5, and undoubtedly elsewhere. But the rule is tricky to apply.

In Conclusion

The *Oil and Gas Journal,* published in Tulsa, Oklahoma, tries to maintain high standards of grammar, idiom, and style without losing its human perspective. Its presentation editor, Max L. Batchelder, has blessed its entire production staff with a memorandum containing these injunctions:

1. Each pronoun should agree with their antecedent.
2. Just between you and I, case is important.
3. Verbs has to agree with their subject.
4. Watch out for irregular verbs that have crope into the language.
5. Don't use no double negatives. Not never.
6. A writer should not shift your point of view.
7. Don't write a run-on sentence you have to punctuate it.
8. About sentence fragments.
9. In articles and stuff like that we use commas to keep things apart without which we would have without doubt confusion.
10. But, don't use, unnecessary commas.
11. It's important to use you're apostrophe's correctly.
12. Don't abbrev. unless nec.
13. Check carefully to if you any words out.
14. In my opinion I think that an author when he is writing something should not gct accustomed to the habit of making use of too many redundant unnecessary words that he does not actually really need in order to put his message across to the reader of the article.
15. About repetition, the repetition of a word is not usually effective repetition.
16. As far as incomplete constructions, they are wrong.
17. Spel correckly.
18. Last but not least, knock off the clichés.

I have never met Mr. Batchelder, but I feel sure I would like him. His admonitions are worth rereading, thinking about, and posting where they are readily visible.

For yourself, be ever alert if you wish to communicate

tellingly and correctly. When you find yourself in doubt about whether or not to utter a particular statement, or about how to express it, ask yourself two questions.

First, which way would be considered traditional among conservative speakers and writers of impeccable taste? If the answer is unsure, try this second question. Which way is most grammatically, idiomatically, or logically consistent? Be guided accordingly.

5

Wellsprings and Reservoirs
—A Communicator's Library

"Some books are to be tasted, others to be
swallowed, and some few to be chewed and
digested. . . ."

—Francis Bacon (Essays, Of Studies)

If you're seriously interested in verbal communication
you will surely keep one or more reference books about it
(at the very least, a dictionary) where you do most of your
reading, writing, or studying. And you will use them
often.

Besides your reference books your verbal communication
will be influenced by other books—texts, novels, and various essays that have shaped your attitudes toward your
language and its culture. Some of these you will certainly
own, and you will occasionally pick up one of them to
reread portions that you especially liked. You may even
enjoy lending them to trusted friends, as I do; and it will

sadden you when one of your books disappears. Other such books you may never own, but you will borrow them from a library or friend, and later return them.

Books are indispensable to verbal communicators, and this book would be incomplete without my own list of favorite and other recommended books, and my comments about those and others. So here they are.

REFERENCE BOOKS

English Dictionaries

Certainly the most generally useful reference tool you can own is a good English dictionary. You will use it most often to check spelling, pronunciation, word division (where to "break" a word when you have too little right margin to complete the word on the same line), and meaning. But you will use it also to check inflectional forms, capitalization, derivation, usage, synonyms, and other things.

Your dictionary will probably serve you more often and influence you more directly than all your other reference books combined. Logically, then, it should be convenient in size and accessibility, genuinely authoritative (not all dictionaries are), and as comprehensive as price and convenience will allow. It may shock you to find what some dictionaries cost, particularly when bought new.

Let's discuss the big ones first. Their bulk makes them inconvenient for desk use, and their cost—unless you can pick up a secondhand bargain—is prohibitive for most individuals.

Surely in terms of scope and scholarship the greatest

English dictionary today is the *Oxford English Dictionary*, published by the Oxford University Press. This is a huge multivolume document that is known affectionately among scholars, researchers, and librarians as "the OED"; it is plainly unsuited to casual use. Besides that, it favors the spelling and pronunciation conventions of Great Britain, which can be disadvantageous in America. However, you should know about the OED. If you're unacquainted with it, ask a librarian to show it to you the next time you visit a large city library. Or you might see one in a large bookstore.

More distinctively American, and usually thought of as "the unabridged" here in the United States, is any edition of the New International series published by the G. & C. Merriam Company in Springfield, Massachusetts. Until 1961 there was little difference of opinion among American teachers, writers, editors, and others concerned for the proper use of English, over which was the "best" American dictionary: it was *Webster's New International Dictionary, Second Edition. Webster II*, as it is commonly called, has long been honored among conservative American professionals.

But in 1961 its publishers introduced *Webster's Third New International Dictionary*, commonly called *Webster III*, which the G. & C. Merriam Company proudly claimed was greatly superior in "scholarship." It introduced a radically different and more complex system for indicating pronunciation and stressing, omitted important reference sections that were included in *Webster II*, and boldly abandoned what it called "prescriptive" lexicography (which helps the user to distinguish between the correct and the incorrect) for what it called "descriptive" lexicography (which reports all words, pronunciations, spellings, and usages that are commonly encountered, without discrimination as to correctness). Thus, *Webster III* is a largely unreliable guide to correct English.

Webster III conspicuously favors the pronunciation of "reduced" (i.e. unstressed) vowel sounds with a kind of *uh* sound represented by an inverted *e* (ə) called the *schwa*. The *Webster III* pronunciation guide suggests that this is the proper sound for the first *a* in banana, the *o* in collect, and the *a* in abut. Do you agree? Neither do I, but that's "scholarship."

Anyway, as a consequence of such things *Webster III* enjoys a disspirited market among dictionary buyers who want sound prescriptive lexicography. Even today, although you can buy a *Webster III* at almost any bookstore, you'll probably pay a considerably higher price for an old *Webster II* if you can find one. Most secondhand bookstores have long waiting lists for *Webster II*.

Therefore, if you want an "unabridged," by all means try to get a *Webster II*, preferably one of the more recent (nearer to 1961) editions. It will lack some of the words that concern electronics and computer technology, and a few others that have crept into our language in recent years, but it will generally give you an authoritative reference to correct English. And if you pay a reasonable price for it you can probably resell it at a profit in any metropolitan city, even to a bookseller.

But few individuals own or need an unabridged dictionary and you will almost certainly prefer one of the smaller books most of the time. At the opposite end of the scale from the OED and the New International series are the paperback or pocket dictionaries, and I cannot honestly recommend any I have seen. Perhaps the best of them are helpful to students by virtue of their conciseness, but they are generally superficial and unsuited to the needs of a business office, for example.

Therefore, I'll confine my remaining remarks about dictionaries to those that are large enough to contain a great fund of information, yet small enough to stand on edge on a desk or hold comfortably on your lap. Most of these range from about two to three inches in thickness, and from about two to four pounds in weight. The better of them cost twelve dollars or more new, but you may be able to find a used one for less.

In my judgment you cannot buy a high quality English dictionary for less than about twelve dollars, and you should look suspiciously at any that are priced—new—at less than ten.

Excellent and reputable dictionaries are published by Random House, Funk & Wagnalls, and others, and I would advise you to visit a high-class bookstore and browse the dictionary shelf. Talk with the owner, if you can; he may be able to tell you knowledgeable opinions expressed by other patrons. But let it be known that you're interested in both prescriptive and descriptive information.

My own favorite is *The American Heritage Dictionary of The English Language* (Houghton Mifflin Company). It's a little larger than some, smaller than others, and delightful to work with. My next-to-favorite, and probably the most convenient physically, is a *Webster's Collegiate Dictionary* (G. & C. Merriam Company) published prior to 1961; that is, an abridgment of *Webster II*. Like *Webster II*, the *Webster's Collegiate* that was abridged from it is out of print; but you can still find used copies in the second-hand book stores.

Thesauri

These are dictionaries of synonyms, and they can be quite helpful when you're looking for a word that means almost but not quite the same thing as another word. But that's all they are really good for. Still, I wouldn't be without mine.

The best-known thesaurus is certainly *Roget's*, published by G. P. Putnam's Sons; you might find it desirable to own one, as I do. Less comprehensive though more analytical is *Crabb's English Synonymes*, published by Routledge & Kegan. It features a kind of "discriminated synonymy" that explains the different connotations or shades of meanings of words that mean almost but not quite the same thing—a most helpful feature that is lacking in *Roget's* and most other comprehensive synonymies.

Possibly the best all-around book of its kind is *Webster's Dictionary of Synonyms* published by the G. & C. Merriam Company, but I would most highly recommend an edition published before 1961. Subsequent editions are descendants of *Webster III*, aforementioned, and are likely to lack valuable prescriptive information.

Style Guides

Style guides are generally intended to establish criteria for the use and formation of written language or for special kinds of writing. There is, of course, no efficiency without discipline, and no discipline without criteria. Style guides offer the criteria, often with helpful ideas beyond what you would expect.

The most widely useful general-purpose style manual is

also the most concise and probably the most widely known: *The Elements of Style*, by William Strunk, Jr. and E. B. White (Macmillan Paperbacks). This is likely to be the least expensive and most enjoyable volume in your reference library. It will give you much sound counsel about the correct use of English, with memorable illustrations.

There is, however, nothing in my experience to equal *A Manual of Style*, published by The University of Chicago Press. It retails for more than twelve dollars, and is worth its price. This is a truly comprehensive style manual. Initially compiled to serve the needs of a university press (its writers, editors, and typesetters), it has become an undisputed general authority among professional communicators in the United States. I could not be entirely happy without my Chicago manual, and I particularly admire its excellent indexing.

Many commercial publishers, some publishing departments in private industry, and some Government agencies have compiled style manuals for their special purposes. Most such manuals are inferior general-purpose reference works; they would have little value to anyone outside their intended offices. There is, however, one Government style guide that every serious communicator should own.

The United States Government Printing Office Style Manual (usually called the *GPO Style Manual*) is probably used more widely by nongovernment than Government communicators, and with good reason. It contains a wealth of both general and special reference information that makes it practically indispensable.

Besides a lot of material that probably will mean nothing to you—data geared to courtwork and the *Congressional Record*, for example—it contains a goldmine of other features that you'll treasure as long as you read and write, including marvelous sections on capitalization, spelling, compounding, punctuation, abbreviations, numerals, tabular work, and (unless you get the special abridged paperback edition) eighteen foreign languages. And it's considered authoritative throughout our Government except where certain agency bureaucrats have established locally variant rules on spelling, capitalizing, or abbreviating.

Many large commercial bookstores keep the *GPO Style Manual* in stock; or you can order it from the Superintendent of Documents, U.S. Government Printing Office, Washington, D.C. 20402. At this writing the buckram edition is $6.70 postpaid (stock #021-000-00068-0); the unabridged paperback is $4.60 postpaid (stock #021-000-00070-1). Make your personal check payable to the Superintendent of Documents, USGPO. It's that simple.

Usage Guides

The one that I most enthusiastically recommend is *The Careful Writer*, by Theodore M. Bernstein, published in hardcover by Atheneum. It's authoritative and concise, informal and entertaining, by a newspaperman who knows grammar, idiom, and style. This is one of the few reference books I know of that you can enjoy casually. That is, you can pick it up and start reading anywhere, and enjoy it and profit by it.

Also available by Mr. Bernstein, and also good (though typographically inferior to *The Careful Writer*, is a paperback entitled *Watch Your Language*, published by Pocket Books (Simon & Schuster, Inc.). A more recent and quite excellent paperback by Mr. Bernstein is called *Miss Thistlebottom's Hobgoblins*, published by Noonday. All three Bernstein books are worthy, but they seem to cover a lot of the same material.

A more classical guide—more scholarly and more comprehensive but less enjoyable to read—is *A Dictionary of Modern English Usage*, by H. W. Fowler, published by Oxford University Press. This is the book of its kind most honored among journalists and scholars, sometimes uncomfortable to work with but always universally respected. Serious students of English idiom should keep it always handy—and quote from it confidently.

Other Reference Books

The list is practically endless, but I'd like to recommend several that I find helpful for general literary purposes, and comment on a few others.

One that I like very well is called *Brewer's Dictionary of Phrase and Fable*, published by Harper & Brothers. Its name is rather apt. In it you can find the origins of thousands of the phrases, fables, and catchwords that have found their way into English idiom and folklore, all conveniently alphabetized. This goes far beyond the dictionary etymologies. When you want to know the antecedents of *cuckold, Daedalus*, or *Jenkin's Ear*, for example, it's a handy book to have. And it will give you a natural filing place for newspaper clippings about such matters that you'll get from time to time.

Perhaps even more valuable to most people is a source of quotations. I like my *Oxford Dictionary of Quotations*, published by the Oxford University Press; but *Bartlett's* is even better known. With such a book you can quickly find apt quotations, alphabetized by subject and by principal word, from most of history's better-known speakers, writers, statesmen, poets, teachers, even the Bible.

And if you're a secretary—maybe even if you're not—you may find a secretary's handbook a valuable accessory to your English dictionary. The one I prefer, among those with which I'm familiar, is called the *Standard Handbook for Secretaries*, by Lois Hutchinson, published by McGraw-Hill Book Company. Besides a lot of business-oriented material on grammar and usage, it contains a wealth of fine reference information concerning numbers, correspondence, forms of address, mail processing, manuscript typing, the keeping of minutes, patents and copyrights, foreign exchange, weights and measures, time, and lots of other data that have to be looked up somewhere—and this is a convenient place.

Then, if you're likely to need authoritative information about etiquette beyond the things you can find in your secretary's handbook, you may want a copy of Amy Vander-bilt's *Complete Book of Etiquette*, published by Doubleday. The Funk & Wagnalls *Etiquette* by Emily Post is still available and still respected, but most of us consider it somewhat outdated in certain matters.

Regarding foreign languages I favor *Cassell's* Latin and French dictionaries published by Funk & Wagnalls, and would favor any others in that series. The typography is excellent.

I own two paperbacks, still in print, that I find very useful, as you might also. The first is a *Dictionary of Foreign Terms*, by C. O. Sylvester Mawson, published by the Thomas Y. Crowell Company. It lists alphabetically thousands of words and phrases from the familar idiom and classical sources of forty-two languages, with special recognition of French, Latin, Spanish, and German, it seems. It's a great convenience in finding quickly the meanings of foreign phrases that certain authors seem to delight in using, as if to remind us that they are smarter than we.

The second of these paperbacks is called *The Concise Dictionary of 26 Languages in Simultaneous Translation*, compiled by Peter M. Bergman and published as a Signet Reference Book by The New American Library. It lists alphabetically 998 common English words and their counterparts in 26 other languages. Following that, it gives alphabetic listings of all 998 words for each of the languages, grouped by language, with page references. It's scholarship is doubtful, I think, and it's more a curiosity than a versatile tool, but I find it useful at times.

Finally, there are the specialty dictionaries: legal, medical, slang, and so on. You'll probably have no need for such books unless you're interested in a vocational field that requires them. But let me offer one bit of advice for the day when you consider buying one.

Try to find a dictionary that will not merely confirm your suspicions about spelling, and tell you what the words mean, but also show you how they should be pronounced. There are some otherwise excellent specialty dictionaries that fall short on that point. When you have to look up a word that's truly strange to you, you need to know how it should be pronounced. Don't get stuck with a dictionary that fails to tell you how.

STUDY BOOKS

The nonreference books that concern language are hard to categorize, so I won't try. It may be unfair to call them study books, for that matter. But the books that I have in

mind are not textbooks in the usual sense of that word, yet
they do deserve deliberate study. I'll mention only three
that I think truly important for basic language study. Beyond those you're on your own.

I believe that no one who knows or senses the impor-
tance of language should fail to read the classical primer
on general semantics, *Language in Thought and Action*,
by S. I. Hayakawa, published by Harcourt Brace Jovano-
vich, Inc. It's well organized, superbly written, and highly
entertaining. This book says so much, and says it both
lightly and profoundly, that you'll probably reread it
periodically through the years, as I do.

Equally interesting, though in a different way, is a book
entitled *The Art of Clear Thinking*,[6] by Rudolf Flesch,
published by Harper & Brothers. Dr. Flesch has written
some excellent books about readable writing, but this one
is not about writing at all—at least, not directly. However,
it tells some things about thinking that bear directly upon
language, and I'm recommending it to you. Like Dr.
Hayakawa's book, it's easy reading, as a book by a professional communicator ought to be.

Finally, and with just a little hesitation, I want to suggest
that you read—or at least sample—a marvelous book
called *The Story of Language*, by Mario Pei; it's available
in paperback as a Mentor Book, published by The New
American Library. It's less light and entertaining than
the two that I mentioned ahead of it, but I believe you'll
love it. You'll love it even more when you discover its
index.

---

6. It's mentioned in the Author's Preface.

Index

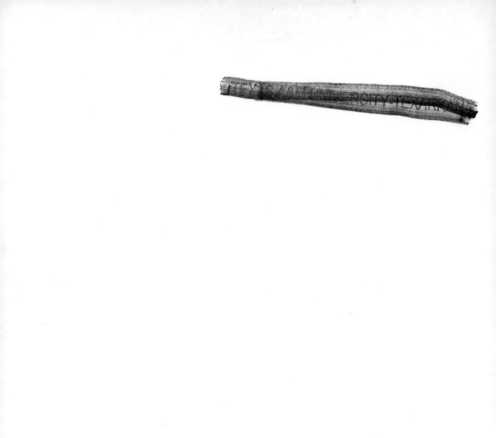